D1520829

PELÉ

Read all of the books in this exciting,
action-packed biography series!

Alex Rodriguez	*Muhammad Ali*
Annika Sorenstam	*Pelé*
Barry Bonds	*Peyton Manning*
Cal Ripken Jr.	*Roberto Clemente*
David Beckham	*Sandy Koufax*
Derek Jeter	*Sasha Cohen*
Doug Flutie	*Tiger Woods*
Hank Aaron	*Tim Duncan*
Ichiro Suzuki	*Tom Brady*
Jesse Owens	*Tony Dungy*
Jim Thorpe	*Wayne Gretzky*
Joe DiMaggio	*Willie Mays*
Josh Gibson	*Wilma Rudolph*
Lance Armstrong	*Wilt Chamberlain*
Michelle Kwan	*Yao Ming*
Mickey Mantle	

PELÉ

by Dax Riner

TF
CB Twenty-First Century Books/Minneapolis

Twenty-First Century Books
A division of Lerner Publishing Group, Inc.
241 First Avenue North
Minneapolis, MN 55401 U.S.A.

Website address: www.lernerbooks.com

Front cover: © Lichfield/Getty Images; AP Photo (background).
Back cover: © Nexus7/Dreamstime.com.

Library of Congress Cataloging-in-Publication Data

Library of Congress Cataloging-in-Publication Data

Riner, Dax.
    Pelé / by Dax Riner.
        p.   cm. — (Sports heroes and legends)
    Includes bibliographical references and index.
    ISBN 978–0–7613–5368–3 (lib. bdg. : alk. paper)
    1. Pelé, 1940—Juvenile literature. 2. Soccer players—Brazil—Biography—Juvenile literature. I. Title.
    GV942.7.P42R56 2011
    796.334092—dc22 [B]   2009035335

Manufactured in the United States of America
1 — VI — 7/15/10

Contents

Prologue

Coming to America

Pelé smiled as he looked out at the crowd. The room at New York City's 21 Club was packed with reporters. Flashbulbs went off left and right. The president of the New York Cosmos, a professional soccer team, announced that his team had signed Pelé to a contract. People around the world were stunned. Why would Pelé play in a country that didn't even care about soccer? The North American Soccer League (NASL) was just five years old. Few Americans even knew it existed. While soccer is said to be the world's most popular sport, in the United States baseball, basketball, and U.S. football are kings. Pelé was determined to change that.

Pelé had retired from soccer a year earlier at the age of thirty-four. But he decided he missed the game too much. The chance to make his mark on U.S. sports was a challenge he couldn't resist, and Clive Toye of the Cosmos knew it. "I told

1

Pelé don't go to Italy, don't go to Spain. All you can do is win a championship. Come to the U.S. and you can win a country," Toye said.

In June 1975, Pelé ran onto the field at Downing Stadium in New York City. The dead grass was spray-painted green, and rocks and broken glass were everywhere. It was a far cry from the beautiful stadiums Pelé was used to playing in. But it didn't matter to the fans. They were there to see Pelé, the king of soccer. Since he hadn't played in a year, Pelé wasn't at his best. But he gave the Downing Stadium crowd a glimpse of the magic that would capture the imagination of sports fans across the country. He dribbled through, past, and around defenders. He made perfect passes to his teammates. Early on, he barely missed scoring when a header bounced off the goalpost. In the second half, Pelé got another chance. This one didn't miss. Twisting in the air, he headed a pass into the net. He jumped and lifted his fist toward the sky in celebration. The crowd went wild, chanting "Pe-lé! Pe-lé!" The excitement would soon sweep across America.

Chapter One

Edson, Dico, Pelé

Edson Arantes do Nascimento was born on October 23, 1940, in Três Corações, Brazil. His parents named him Edson in tribute to Thomas Edison, the inventor of electricity. Of course, Edson is now known as Pelé, one of the world's greatest soccer players. But he would not get his more famous nickname until he was older. Pelé was not born in a hospital. He was born in his parents' small brick house. His father, Dondinho, was a professional soccer player. He was in the army when he met Celeste, Pelé's mother. Pelé was the couple's first child.

> ❝I was born in a town called Three Hearts. I tell everybody I am a man of three hearts. That means I'm going to last 200 years.❞
>
> —Pelé

When Pelé was born, Dondinho looked at his son's tiny legs and smiled. "This one will be a great soccer player," he said. Celeste thought it was just one of Dondinho's crazy dreams. She'd seen what soccer had done to her husband. His knees were so bad that he walked with a permanent limp. Celeste didn't want that for her firstborn son, whom she called "Dico."

The family was very poor. Although Dondinho was a very good player, he didn't make much money. Soccer-crazy Brazil had a lot of very good players. Celeste wanted her husband to find a job that paid better, especially since their family was growing. Dondinho looked for other work, but soccer was his greatest love. It was hard for him to give it up.

In 1945, when Pelé was four years old, his father got an offer to play for a team in Bauru, Brazil. The team had also arranged a government job for Dondinho. Celeste felt better knowing her husband would have stable, better-paying work. The family of five (Pelé now had a brother, Jair, and a sister, Maria Lucia) boarded a train for Bauru and their new life. "My first real memory begins with the train ride to Bauru," Pelé said. He also remembered leaning out the window to get a better view, which made his mom very angry.

Pelé spent the train ride watching the ever-changing scenery. It was the first time he'd been outside of Três Corações. When the train arrived in Bauru, Pelé was amazed at the size of the city. It had every kind of shop imaginable. It even had a

4

movie theater! The family felt that their life together was taking a turn for the better. But sadly, the good feelings didn't last long. By the time Pelé's family arrived in Bauru, the government job Dondinho had been promised was no longer part of the deal.

It was a difficult time. The family was in a strange, new city with little money. Dondinho struggled to support his family. "As I grew up, I began to learn what poverty was," Pelé said. It was a tough life, but the family was close. Pelé said, "There was a great deal of love in that small house. Love that overcame much of the hardship." Hardship included a house without heat and a leaking roof. On cold nights, the family gathered in the kitchen to stay warm. But despite everything, Pelé enjoyed Bauru, the place where he first fell in love with soccer. From sunrise to sunset, Pelé was in the streets, kicking a ball around with his friends. Not a real ball, however. They didn't have money for that. They used a rolled-up sock stuffed with rags. It was nothing fancy, but Pelé didn't care. "The pleasure of kicking that ball, making it move, was the greatest feeling of power I had ever had up to that time."

Dondinho saw the interest his son had in soccer. He spent a lot of time with Pelé, teaching him what he knew about the game. But Celeste wasn't happy. A lot of kids dreamed of playing soccer professionally, but few of them ever did. She didn't want her son's life to be full of struggle and broken dreams. Celeste was a small woman with a beautiful smile. But she was tough too. She was the boss of the household, and she made sure her children behaved. "We didn't steal, we didn't beg, we didn't lie, we didn't cheat," Pelé said. "We treated people older than ourselves with respect. And above all, we obeyed our parents."

Celeste knew the importance of education. She tried to make sure Pelé did his homework and studied. But Pelé struggled in school. He liked to talk in class, which often meant he got punished. And when he wasn't in class, Pelé didn't give school much thought. What he did think about was soccer, from morning till night. To avoid doing homework, Pelé got a job as a shoeshine boy. It took him a week to get his first customer. But he stuck with the job and earned some money.

In 1948, when Pelé was eight, his father finally got the job he'd been promised. After work, he'd spend time with Pelé. The two became very close. Dondinho would tell his son stories about his life as a soccer player. Pelé listened eagerly and soon decided he wanted to be a soccer player, just like his dad. When Pelé listened to games on the radio, he was fascinated by the announcers as they described the exploits of the star players. Pelé dreamed that one day people would hear his name on the radio too.

When Pelé was ten, he got the name that is now known around the world. How he got the name Pelé or who gave it to him remains a mystery—even to Pelé. "They say it just began one day, and after that it stuck because it seemed to fit, whatever it means." At first, Pelé hated the name. He'd even get into fights with other kids over it. But it was no use. "I must have lost most of them, because the name stuck!" he said. But not everyone used the new name. At home, Pelé was still known as Dico. And he still is, to this day.

FIRST SHOES

When Pelé was ten, he got his first pair of shoes from his aunt Maria. Pelé was only supposed to wear the shoes to church. But one time, he wore them to play soccer. "I had to know how it felt to kick a ball with shoes on," he said. Needless to say, his mom was not happy!

By this time, Pelé was the best soccer player of the kids his age. He wanted a challenge. So he began playing with older kids. After a while, they formed a team. They named the team September 7, after Brazil's independence day. The team didn't have a real ball, uniforms, or even cleats. The kids tried all sorts of things to raise money for shoes. But nothing worked. Finally, they changed their name to The Shoeless Ones. They managed to raise enough money to buy a ball. Pelé was the team's captain, so he got to keep the ball at his house.

Dondinho was happy that his son loved soccer. He spent many hours coaching Pelé. And Pelé often went to watch his dad play. One time, a fan yelled at Dondinho for missing a shot. Pelé got angry and almost got into a fight with the other fan. Later, at home, Dondinho took Pelé aside. He told Pelé that if he wanted to be a pro player, he would have to learn to control his temper. Pelé nodded. He promised himself he'd never lose his temper on the field.

In 1952, the father of one of Pelé's friends offered to coach The Shoeless Ones. He said he could get them soccer shoes. The boys quickly agreed, and soon they had their shoes. But now they needed a new name for the team. They chose Ameriquinha, which means "Little America." Little America had never played on grass. They'd always played on city streets. But they entered a tournament run by Bauru's mayor and played their first game on grass. Pelé loved it!

Little America made it to the finals. Pelé was confident his team would win. "We knew how to play soccer on the streets without shoes, without a ball. And there we were, playing on a comfortable field covered with beautiful grass. Why wouldn't we win?"

When Pelé scored the winning goal, the crowd began to chant "Pelé! Pelé!" The nickname Pelé once hated now didn't sound so bad after all! Dondinho was in the stands when twelve-year-old Pelé scored that goal. After the game, he hugged his son tightly and told him, "You played a beautiful game. I couldn't have played better myself." At home, Celeste smiled at the news that her son was the star player. Pelé felt very proud. "That was the first time I saw her happy about soccer."

For winning the tournament, Little America got 36 cruzeiros (about 1 cent in 2009 U.S. dollars). Usually the players divided up the money. But since Pelé had scored the winning goal, his teammates insisted he take it all. When Celeste found out, she made Pelé give the other players back their money. She told her son that no single player was more valuable than any other. It was another important lesson for the young player.

Pelé felt on top of the world. His dream of becoming a professional soccer player didn't seem so crazy after all. But then three of Little America's players moved away and so did the team's coach. Little America couldn't find any new players or a new coach. Pelé wondered what he would do without a team.

Chapter Two

One Step Closer

After Little America broke up, Pelé was worried. He needed a team if he was going to continue toward his goal of being a professional soccer player. Luckily, he soon found a new team. His father played for the Bauru Athletic Club, or BAC. BAC had recently formed a youth team called Little BAC. It wasn't long before Pelé was playing for them.

Little BAC's coach would play an important role in Pelé's life. Valdemar De Brito played on Brazil's 1934 World Cup team. He'd also coached Pelé's father. De Brito was an excellent teacher. He helped Pelé strengthen his game, especially heading the ball. You can't use your hands in soccer, so using your head to hit the ball is an important skill.

De Brito enjoyed teaching youngsters. To him, one player in particular had the makings of a star—Pelé. "Of all the players, only one stood out. I immediately spotted what can be called genius,"

De Brito said. But De Brito also missed the excitement of the big city. He soon took another job, in his Brazilian hometown of São Paulo. Pelé was disappointed, but then Radium, another Bauru team, asked him to join. Pelé happily agreed. At the age of fourteen, Pelé was the youngest player on the team. He was also the only nonprofessional player. It said a lot about Pelé's abilities that he was asked to play with older men.

Pelé led the league with forty goals in his first season with Radium. He was also making waves at home—and not in a good way. Although he worked hard, Pelé continued to struggle in school. With his mother's help, Pelé finally managed to finish school. After graduation he worked in a shoe factory. But his dream of playing professional soccer was still burning brightly.

Pelé was quickly making a name for himself. A coach from a team in the big city of Rio de Janiero came to see him. In 1954, he offered Pelé a spot on his team. Pelé was overcome with excitement. He'd be able to realize his dream of playing in the Maracanã, Rio's world-famous stadium.

Pelé asked his father for permission, and Dondinho said he could go. But Pelé's mother also had to agree. Nervously, Pelé asked her if he could go to Rio. Celeste said no. She thought it was too early for her fourteen-year-old son to leave home. Pelé was upset, but he refused to give up. He worked hard to improve his game. Another chance would come, he thought.

11

BICYCLE KICK

While Pelé did not invent one of the most famous kicks in soccer, he certainly perfected it. The bicycle kick is when a player kicks the ball in midair backward and over his or her own head, usually making contact above waist level. It gets its name from the player's legs, which look as if they are pedaling a bicycle.

In 1955, that chance came. Pelé's old coach, Valdemar De Brito, paid Pelé's father a visit. De Brito knew the president of Santos, a professional team in the city of the same name. He told Dondinho that he could get Pelé a spot on the junior team. Dondinho was excited, but Celeste was still unsure. De Brito reassured Pelé's mother and told her he would personally watch out for Pelé. Celeste still said no. "He's still my baby," she said.

De Brito didn't give up. A week later, he urged Celeste to talk to the president of the Santos team. She didn't know what good it would do, but she agreed. After she got off the phone with the team president, Celeste changed her mind. She said she'd let Pelé go to Santos. She'd seen her husband devote his life to soccer and have little to show for it. But she also knew that soccer might be her son's only chance out of a life of poverty. "I don't want to see you sewing shoes for the rest of your life," she told Pelé.

Santos was about the same size as Bauru, which helped Celeste feel more comfortable about her son leaving. But there was one big difference between the two cities—Santos was by the Atlantic Ocean. Bauru was an inland city, so Pelé had never seen the sea.

The family got Pelé ready for his journey. Celeste wanted to make sure her son was dressed for the occasion. She insisted he get new clothes. The family scraped together enough money to get Pelé some shirts and shoes.

At last, Pelé was ready. Dressed in his new clothes, he boarded the train with his father. He was excited but nervous. He didn't know what to expect in a new city, far from his family and friends. He wondered if he was good enough to succeed as a soccer player. He thought about the promise he'd made to his parents, that he would buy them a house as soon as he had the money. "Don't dream just yet," his father had told him. The words filled Pelé's head as he tried to sleep.

De Brito, Pelé's old coach, met Pelé and his father at the station in São Paulo. Then the three of them took the bus to Santos. As the bus traveled through São Paulo, Pelé gazed out the window in amazement. He'd never seen so many tall buildings! When the bus left the city, the view changed to green jungles and dramatic cliffs. As Pelé stared at the scenery, De Brito tried to prepare the teenager for his new team. "Don't be awed by the stars playing for Santos," De Brito said. "The people there are great and will help you." Pelé felt lucky to have such a caring person looking out for him.

BRAZIL AND RACE

Brazil's diverse population is made up of several ethnic groups, including people descended from European and from African backgrounds. Unfortunately, racism has long been a problem in Brazil. In general, European-descended people are wealthier and have higher social status than Afro-Brazilians. Pelé's father played at a time when Afro-Brazilian players were kept off the big-city and national teams. Luckily for Pelé, attitudes about race in Brazil—at least in sports—had begun to change by the time he began playing professionally.

At last, the bus pulled into Santos. But before Pelé went to see his new team, he wanted to do one thing. Since he was a little boy, he'd dreamed of seeing the sea. So his father and De Brito took him to the beach. Pelé stared at the blue water and picked up handfuls of sand. Finally, Pelé took one more look at the ocean before heading back to the city and his new life.

Chapter | Three

Santos

After leaving the beach, Pelé's next stop was to watch his new team. Santos was playing in the São Paulo championship at the local stadium. Inside, Pelé was astonished by the number of people and the level of noise. Growing up, Pelé was a fan of the Corinthians, a São Paulo team that was one of the most popular and successful in the country. But from this day forward, his loyalty would be with Santos.

Santos did not disappoint its newest fan—and player. They won the game, sending the fans into a frenzy. Pelé, Dondinho, and De Brito went to the locker room. Pelé stood in awe. The coach spotted the starry-eyed teen and walked over to greet him. "So you're the famous Pelé, eh?" he asked. Pelé shook his hand and smiled. One by one, the Santos players came over to say hello. Pelé had been worried that the older players would be mean or would treat him like a child. But here he was, shaking

hands with the stars he'd heard so much about on the radio—
Jair, Zito, Pepe, Vaconcelos.

A little while later, it was time for De Brito and Dondinho to leave. Pelé had dreaded this moment. Although everyone seemed nice, Pelé was not looking forward to being on his own. He was in a strange city where he didn't know anybody. Who would he talk to? Who would support him? Dondinho could see the worry in his son's eyes. "Don't worry. You'll be all right," he said. The two hugged and Dondinho was gone, on his way back to Bauru.

With an empty feeling in his stomach, Pelé was shown his new home—a large room beneath the stadium's stands. Seven other players lived there too. The room wasn't fancy, but it was comfortable. The other boys were friendly and welcoming, so Pelé soon relaxed. If he couldn't be with his family, at least he was with these nice people. Maybe he could make some new friends. And the next day he'd get to play soccer, which always cheered him up.

Santos had three teams: one team for players sixteen years old and younger, another for players between seventeen and twenty years old, and the main team, which was the one with the best players. At fifteen years old, Pelé thought he'd practice with the players his own age. But before his first practice, Pelé got a big surprise. The coach came over and told Pelé he'd be practicing with the main team. "They threw me in at the deep end," he later said. As Pelé got dressed, he was so nervous his legs were shaking. Pepe, one of the older players, tried to comfort him. "Don't be nervous," Pepe said. "The guys are great. You'll see."

When Pelé ran onto the field, all his nervousness disappeared. On the field, there was no time to worry or feel sad. He'd been playing against older men for years. "Little by little, I gained confidence and even asked for passes and tried to dribble to score," he said. Pelé played center forward and had a great practice. Everyone was impressed. The coach congratulated Pelé. But he also told Pelé that he was too skinny. He said that Pelé would have to get stronger if he wanted to make the main team. With the coach's words ringing in his ears, Pelé spent hours working out. He ate larger meals so he'd put on weight. He was determined to do whatever was needed. Later, he said, "I knew I really had to apply myself if I was going to get anywhere."

Pelé's hard work started to pay off. He continued playing with the junior teams but practicing with the main team. He led the twenty-and-younger team to its league title. The sixteen-and-younger team also made it to their league championship. They wanted Pelé too, and Pelé jumped at the chance. But this time, things didn't work out nearly as well. The game was close. Both teams were strong and well coached. Then Santos caught a break when they were given a penalty shot by the referee. The coach chose Pelé to take the shot. Pelé was nervous. He waited as the referee put the ball down and stepped back. Pelé looked at the ball, then at the goalkeeper. The crowd got louder and louder. Finally, the referee blew his whistle. Pelé ran toward the ball and gave it a good hard kick. The ball sailed toward the goal—and over the crossbar. Pelé couldn't believe it. He'd missed! The fans groaned and then began to boo. They booed louder when Santos lost the game. Pelé couldn't help but feel the loss was his fault. He was humiliated. He decided he would leave Santos. He was too ashamed to stay.

That night, Pelé slept poorly. He tossed and turned, replaying the missed shot in his mind. He got out of bed before sunrise and quietly got dressed and packed his bag. He wondered what his parents would say when he was back in Bauru. Pelé was almost out the door when he heard a voice. "Where do you think you're going?" It was Sabuzinho, a man who worked for the team. Lying, Pelé said he had written permission to go. He just had to go pick up the document. But Sabuzinho wasn't fooled. "Go back to your room," he said. "If you try running away again, I'll have to take your suitcase away from you." Defeated, Pelé hung his head. He was even sadder than before. He couldn't even run away right. But then Sabuzinho said something that connected with the young Pelé. "Everyone makes mistakes once in a while," Sabuzinho said. "The trick is to learn from them, not give in to them." Sure, the penalty shot hadn't turned out the way Pelé had hoped. But that's how life went sometimes. Pelé decided right then that he wouldn't give in or give up. He'd keep working to get better and better and make everyone forget about that missed penalty shot.

Pelé went in as offensive midfielder during a practice with the main team. With the younger teams, he'd been a supporting midfielder, helping out on defense and setting up the forwards for their offensive attacks. Now he'd have a chance to be one of the attackers and score goals. It was a chance to show his magic!

But two other men were also trying out for midfielder. Both of them were excellent players, and making the main team wouldn't be easy. "As I watched them play, I thought my own chance would be a long time coming," Pelé said. Luck again would shine on Pelé, however. Santos had a practice game in a nearby city. The team didn't want to risk all their stars getting hurt in a game that didn't count, so Pelé was chosen as one of the replacement players. For the first time, Pelé pulled on the black-and-white Santos jersey. He ran onto the field filled with confidence. When the game was over, Santos had scored six goals—and Pelé had scored four of them!

THE BEAUTIFUL GAME

Pelé calls soccer "the beautiful game." Only in the United States is it called "soccer." Everywhere else in the world, it's called football. Calling soccer the beautiful game was Pelé's way of explaining to Americans the difference between soccer and American football.

Because it was a practice game, the goals didn't count toward his career total. But to Pelé, they were as important as any he'd ever scored. "I could tell that the other players looked at me slightly differently afterwards," he said. "It was as if they were beginning to understand why I'd been let onto the team so young." With each day that passed, Pelé felt more comfortable in Santos. His comfort showed on the field too. In his first season, he led the league in scoring, even though he didn't play in every game. Pelé's exceptional play was starting to attract a lot of attention. One group of people was especially interested—the leaders of Brazil's national team.

Chapter | Four

World Cup

Soccer teams from all over the world compete in the World Cup, a three-week-long tournament whose winner is named world champion. Like the Olympics, the World Cup is held once every four years in a different country each time. In 1958, Sweden hosted the World Cup. Pelé hoped his performance for Santos would pay off with a spot on Brazil's team. But he knew few players his age played in such a huge tournament. After all, only the best in the world played in the World Cup. Still, Pelé was hopeful.

One day, Pelé's father called. He was listening to the radio when they announced who would be invited to try out for the Brazilian squad. Dondinho thought Pelé's name was one of the names he heard. But he wasn't *completely* sure. There was a Brazilian player named Telê, which sounded a lot like "Pelé."

Pelé waited to see if someone would tell him he'd been selected, but he grew anxious and decided to try and find out on his own. He asked his teammates, but they hadn't heard anything. Pelé headed upstairs to the team offices. He found Modesto Roma, the Santos chairman. "Have I been invited?" Pelé asked Roma. Roma's answer sent Pelé's heart racing. "Hey, kiddo, you've made the *Seleção*." The Seleção, or the "Selection," was a group of players from whom Brazil's team would be chosen. More names were on the Seleção list than spots on the team, and this meant there was still a chance that Pelé might not go to Sweden. So while Pelé was pleased, he was still worried.

At last the day arrived. All the players gathered to learn who would wear the yellow-and-green uniform of Brazil's World Cup team. Everyone was nervous. One by one, the names were read off. Pelé's name wasn't one of them. His heart sank. But then he was told the names were of those who had *not* made the team. At seventeen, Pelé would play in the World Cup!

Before the Brazilian team went to Sweden, they played an exhibition game. The group hadn't played together before, so the exhibition gave them a chance to get to know one another better. The game was against the Corinthians, which had once been Pelé's favorite team. It was a hard-fought game, even if it didn't count. At one point, Pelé got the ball. He dribbled toward the Corinthians' goal. Suddenly, a defender dove for the ball.

Pelé tried to dodge him. But the defender's foot struck Pelé's right knee. Pelé collapsed in agony.

The team doctor rushed onto the field. He asked Pelé if he could keep playing. The pain was incredible. But Pelé knew that if he was hurt, he might not go to Sweden. "Yes, I can go on," he told the doctor. But when Pelé tried to put his weight on his leg, the knee gave way. Pelé limped to the sidelines, sad and disappointed. On the bench, the doctor put ice on Pelé's knee. He tried to reassure Pelé. "You'll be fine," the doctor said. But Pelé wasn't so sure. That night, his knee still hurt badly. In the morning, he went to see the head of the Brazilian team. Pelé didn't want to be a burden. He said he would step aside so a healthy player could go to Sweden. But Pelé was told not to worry. Everyone thought he'd heal in time for the World Cup. Relieved, Pelé went home and slept.

The Brazilian team went to Italy for some warm-up games. The trip was Pelé's first time on a plane. Wide-eyed, he stared out the window and took in everything he saw. The players joked and played games to pass the time, which helped Pelé forget all about his knee. At last, the plane landed in Rome. The team took a bus tour of the city's famous sites. Pelé could hardly believe that at the age of seventeen he was in Europe, traveling with the team he'd idolized as a young boy!

Pelé was anxious to play, but the team was worried about his knee. They didn't want him to hurt it worse. So Pelé sat on the bench for the two games in Italy. Then it was back on the plane for the flight to Sweden. Out his window, Pelé marveled at the views of the snow-covered Alps. He'd seen mountains in Brazil, but none as tall as these! Finally, the plane landed in Sweden. The lakes were clear blue, the trees were tall and green, and the air was crisp and clean. Pelé felt very lucky. Soccer not only made him happy—it was letting him see the world.

In the days leading up to Brazil's first game, the players were getting along well. Everyone was relaxed, but they were also focused on their goal. They knew how hard it was to win the World Cup. Pelé felt the team was well prepared and in great shape. He had no doubt Brazil could win it all. His only worry was his injured knee.

❝*The rule one must live one's life by is to respect other people, whoever they are.*❞

—Pelé

In Pelé's first World Cup game, he watched Brazil beat Austria 3–0. Three days later, Brazil played England. The team doctor decided it was still too early for Pelé to test his knee. So he was on the bench again. It was a tough game. England's defense was determined to stop Brazil's strong offense. Brazil had some chances, but England's goalkeeper was up to the challenge. The game ended in a 0–0 tie. Pelé was frustrated. If he had played, he might have made the difference.

Only one more game was in the first round of the 1958 World Cup. The Brazilians needed to win to make sure they advanced to the second round. It wouldn't be easy. Brazil had to play the Soviet Union, one of the favorites to win the tournament. During warm-ups, Pelé looked across the field at the Soviet players. They were huge! But Pelé wasn't afraid. "Big trees can be chopped down too," he thought. By now, Pelé was going crazy. He was no longer satisfied just to be on the team. He wanted to play! His knee was improving. In practice, he felt great and played well. The day before the game against the Soviets, the coach asked Pelé if he was ready. Enthusiastically, Pelé said, "Yes!"

On June 15, 1958, Pelé ran onto the field's green grass. He was the youngest player in the World Cup. He smiled and imagined what the fifty thousand fans were thinking as they watched him, a boy among men. Maybe they thought he was a mascot or the coach's son. Pelé would soon teach them how wrong they were. When the Brazilian national anthem played, Pelé was overcome with pride. "My thoughts went back to Brazil. I could imagine my whole family listening on the radio," he said. All the practice and all the pain had paid off.

From the start, the Brazilians were on top of their game. Again and again they attacked the Soviets' goal. First Garrincha and then Pelé took shots that hit the crossbar. Pelé bowed his head in frustration. His teammate Didi ran over. "Relax, kid, the goal will come. Take it easy," he said. Didi's words rang true not long after. Didi made a perfect pass to Vavá, who ripped a shot past the Soviet goalkeeper. Brazil was ahead 1–0.

As the game went on, Pelé's knee got more and more sore. He tried to hide his limp, afraid he'd be taken out. He couldn't remember ever feeling so anxious during a game. Later, Pelé got another chance to score, but he shot the ball wide. Pelé was sure he would have scored a goal if he had been more relaxed. The Soviets grew more desperate. In the second half, they came at the Brazilians with everything they had. But the Soviets just couldn't put the tying goal in the net. The Brazilians' tension grew. The game seemed like it would never end! Then Vavá broke free and scored his second goal. The Brazilian players celebrated wildly, more out of relief than anything else. A two-goal lead was much easier to protect. When the whistle finally blew, Pelé threw up his arms in happiness. Brazil was going on to the next round. That night, the team got together for a big celebration dinner, but Pelé went back to his room early. He couldn't stop thinking about the game. He wished he'd played better. He promised himself he'd learn from his mistakes.

Two days later, Brazil played Wales. Pelé was determined to make up for his mediocre game against the Soviet Union. The first half was rough. The Welsh defense stood their ground, and the Brazilians couldn't break through. At halftime, the score was 0–0. In the second half, Pelé made his mark—the first of many in World Cup play. With his back to the Welsh goal, Pelé took a pass from Didi. Pelé trapped the ball perfectly with his chest. The ball fell to his right foot as he turned past the defender. Pelé then sent a low drive toward the goal. The Welsh goalie dove for the ball. Pelé was sure he'd make the save. But the ball bounced off a Welsh defender and rolled into the net! Pelé ran across the field, jumping and yelling. "I have no idea how many times I ran and jumped, ran and jumped, all the while screaming, 'Goal!' like a maniac." Pelé's first World Cup goal had won the game! "It was one of the most important goals I ever scored," he said. "Not one of the best, but it settled me. Calmed me."

Brazil was in the semifinals. They traveled to Stockholm, Sweden, to battle France. Early on, Brazil looked like it would run away with the game. Vavá scored in the opening moments for a 1–0 lead. But France came right back to tie the score. The goal was the first Brazil had allowed in the 1958 World Cup. Pelé grabbed the ball out of the net and ran to the center circle. "Let's stop wasting time. Let's get started!" he shouted. The rest of the team looked at him in amazement. They didn't expect such a show from a teenager. Just before the end of the half, a Didi blast put Brazil up 2–1. But the second half belonged to the seventeen-year-old from Bauru. In just over twenty minutes, Pelé scored three goals. The third was spectacular—a volley from the edge of the penalty box. With its 5–2 win, Brazil moved on to the finals against Sweden.

Pelé and his teammates knew the Swedes would be a tough test. They were playing in their own country in front of their own fans. That gave Sweden a strong advantage. But Pelé had come too far to go home disappointed. As the Brazilian national anthem played before the final match, Pelé looked toward the sky. He had never felt more proud. Trembling, he thought of his father back in Bauru, listening on his radio. He knew his mom would stay out of the room, determined not to listen. But he knew as soon as the game was over, she'd ask her husband all about what had happened.

Pelé's mom never saw her son play in person until his last game. She'd seen her husband get badly hurt in a game, and she was afraid the same thing would happen to Pelé. She couldn't bear to see her son get hurt, so she stayed away from his games.

Pelé's pride turned sour early in the game. Four minutes in, Sweden went ahead 1–0. For the first time in the 1958 tournament, Brazil was behind. Some had wondered how the team would react to the pressure. Now everyone would find out. Instead of feeling tense, Pelé felt strangely calm, and he didn't fight the feeling. His teammates must have felt the same way. Just five minutes later, Brazil tied the game. Then they took the lead on Vavá's second goal of the game. But just as he had against France, Pelé performed well in the second half. And his show of skill was not one that would soon be forgotten.

Ten minutes into the second half, Pelé took a pass with his back to the Swedish goal. With a defender on him, Pelé trapped the ball with his thigh and turned around. Another defender rushed toward him. But Pelé flicked the ball up and over the charging Swede. Just before the ball hit the ground, Pelé kicked it past the goalkeeper. Goal! Pelé leaped and raised his fist with a shout.

Near the end of the match, a teammate sent a pass through the air. Rushing toward the Swedish goal, Pelé jumped high, rising above two defenders. With his head, Pelé flicked the ball up and over the goalkeeper's reaching hands. The amazing goal put the game away. When the game was over, Pelé felt lightheaded. He thought he might faint. He couldn't believe Brazil had won! He wondered if his parents were listening at home. Did they know their son was a World Cup champion? Suddenly, Pelé was surrounded by his teammates. They picked up their youngest player and carried him on their shoulders. Tears of happiness filled Pelé's eyes. One player, Gilmar, reached up and squeezed Pelé's leg. "Go ahead and cry," he told Pelé. "It's good for you!"

By tradition, the World Cup winners take a victory lap around the stadium. The Brazilians did just that, waving their flag as they ran in triumph. Some other players grabbed a Swedish flag and held it up too. The king of Sweden came down to shake hands with the Brazilian team. Even the Swedish player who guarded Pelé was in awe. "After the fifth goal, even *I* wanted to cheer for Pelé," Sigge Parling said. That night, the team had a celebratory dinner and party at the hotel. But Pelé skipped the party. He was exhausted and went to bed instead.

The next day, the Brazilians boarded a plane for the long flight home. Pelé couldn't wait to see his parents. Hours later, the plane arrived in Rio de Janeiro. Huge crowds greeted the bus at every stop. Cars honked. People shouted and fireworks crackled in the air. The scene was unlike anything Pelé had ever seen. The players climbed on the back of fire trucks and rode through the city. People were everywhere, cheering their hearts out! Later, the players got a pleasant surprise. When they went to the office of a local magazine for a party, they found their parents waiting. The magazine owners had paid to bring the players' parents to Rio! Pelé rushed toward his mom and dad. The three shared a long hug and more tears of joy.

The team spent the next few days traveling from town to town. Everywhere they went, they were greeted by enthusiastic crowds. There were more parades and dinners and parties. Reporters asked question after question. Pelé knew Brazilians loved soccer, but he never realized how much. He was proud to have helped make so many so happy. The tour of Brazil was fun, but after a while, Pelé just wanted to be with his family. Finally, he got his wish. The tour ended at last, and Pelé boarded a plane for Bauru.

Two years earlier, Pelé had been a scared teenager leaving home for the first time. Now he was returning as a champion—and a star. Reporters mobbed him as he stepped off the plane. People were everywhere, shouting his name. "I began to feel the excitement building up in me as I hadn't felt it before," he said. "This was my home." As he rode through town, he thought about the tough times of his childhood. Of shining shoes, playing in the streets, and stealing peanuts. It seemed like yesterday. And yet it also seemed so long ago. Then Pelé looked up and saw a banner. The words made him more proud than he'd ever felt. "Welcome, Pelé," it read. "Son of Bauru, champion of the world."

Chapter Five

A National Treasure

To honor Pelé, Bauru's mayor put up a stand in the town center. Thousands of people turned out to see their hometown hero. Pelé received gifts, trophies, and more. He even got a car, although he was too young to drive! The car was nothing fancy—a three-wheeled model that was popular at the time. Pelé wasn't even sure the car would make it to Santos. But he was thankful and honored to receive such a gift. The next day, Pelé decided to give the car to his parents. He didn't have a license, and he wanted to show his parents his appreciation for all their support.

Pelé thought his dad would be happy. But he was surprised by his father's reaction. Dondinho told his son that it wasn't right to give away something he'd been given. The two argued. Neither would give in. Finally, Celeste said it wouldn't be safe for their eighteen-year-old son to drive in the city. This changed

Dondinho's mind. But he said he'd only keep the car for Pelé until he was old enough to take it back.

Thanks to the World Cup win, Pelé was a national hero. But he didn't feel much different than he had before the tournament. People were amazed that the fame didn't go to his head. Not Pelé. "I was still me, just me, living in Santos with my friends and doing what I loved to do—playing soccer."

As a young boy, Pelé's soccer hero was Brazilian Zizinho. In 1957, seventeen-year-old Pelé played against Zizinho for the first time. Zizinho was impressed. "Pelé fought like a real warrior for the whole match. I liked his technical qualities tremendously and those that go beyond the sport, too. I thought he'd go far. And I wasn't wrong."

With all the celebrations over, Pelé rejoined Santos. He picked up where he'd left off. In thirty-eight games, he scored an incredible fifty-eight goals. Then he helped Santos win the 1958 São Paulo championship. For Pelé, one game stood out from the rest, but not because of what happened on the field.

In September 1958, Santos was set to play the Corinthians. The night before the game, the Santos players were restless.

Pelé suggested they go watch a girls' basketball game to unwind. One of the basketball players immediately caught Pelé's eye. When the game was over, the girl walked up to him. "You're Pelé, right?" she asked. Pelé was pleased that she knew who he was. But his happiness didn't last long. The girl said she hoped Santos lost to the Corinthians and then walked away. Afterward, Pelé couldn't stop thinking about her. During the soccer game the next day, he kept looking into the stands. He was sure she'd be there. But if she was, Pelé didn't see her.

Time passed. Then one day Pelé ran into some of the girls on the street and found out the girl's name—Rose. He also found out where she worked. He went straight there but stopped outside the door. He was nervous. Finally, Pelé worked up the courage to go inside. He asked Rose out on a date. She accepted. On the day of their date, Pelé shined his shoes and got dressed in his best clothes. He went to Rose's house to pick her up. He was nervous about meeting her parents. But once he met them, he felt right at home. Her dad was a big soccer fan, and her mother welcomed him happily. "I felt that sense of family again, like with my own parents," Pelé said. He and Rose spent a lot of time together. After the couple had only been dating for a few months, Pelé began to think about marriage.

But first Pelé had to deal with the army. In Brazil, all boys must serve in the armed forces for one year once they turn eighteen. Pelé hoped he could get out of his obligation. He figured his service on the national soccer team was good enough. Pelé went to Santos's team leaders to plead his case. "I've already fought for my country," he said. "Surely I don't need to go to the army to do so again." The men just laughed. "You've just won the World Cup. The whole country knows you are a shining example of health. If there is any eighteen-year-old Brazilian who has to do military service, then it's you," one of the men said. There was no way out. And so Pelé did his duty and joined the army. He was allowed to keep playing for Santos while he served as a soldier, but two jobs made for a very busy life for a teenager!

Pelé's commanding officer was Colonel Osman. The colonel was a big soccer fan, but Pelé didn't want the other soldiers to think he was getting special treatment. He washed clothes and shined shoes, just like everyone else. "It was tough, but I had my duty and I was going to go through it just like the other soldiers," he said. Pelé thought being in the army would cut into his soccer. But he was playing more soccer than ever. He joined an army team that played other army teams from the area. He was also picked to play in the South American Military Championship. In the finals against Argentina, Pelé achieved another first. But this one wasn't quite so special. The game was rough. Pelé was constantly kicked and grabbed. Finally, he'd had enough. The next time Pelé got kicked, he kicked back. A fight broke out. For the first time in his life, Pelé was taken out of a game.

When Pelé's army service was completed, he went back to his regular life. At first, he hadn't been excited to join the army. But he eventually realized it was a worthwhile experience. Pelé went back to Santos. He needed to sign a new contract with the team. Pelé was one of soccer's brightest young stars, and he'd helped Brazil win the World Cup. So he got a large raise in pay. He used the money to pay off his parents' house.

By 1959, Santos was one of Brazil's best teams. To take advantage of their team's success, the bosses scheduled tours of South America and Europe. The travel never seemed to stop. Having a day off was rare. In 1959, Pelé played 103 games for five teams. He once played three games in two days! "It was ridiculous," Pelé said. "There was no time to relax. There was hardly enough time to travel from stadium to stadium!"

In 1960, things slowed down a little. Pelé and his team-mates actually had time to sightsee when they were in Europe. In Egypt, Pelé visited the pyramids and rode a camel. Still, the schedule was grueling. In 1961, Pelé turned twenty-one. Despite playing in numerous games, Pelé had managed to avoid serious injury. But during a game in Mexico City, his luck changed. While going up for a header, Pelé got hit in the face. He was knocked out cold. The doctors quickly revived Pelé, and he wanted to keep playing. But as soon as he stood up, he fell down again. Pelé was helped off the field. His day was over.

That night, Pelé couldn't sleep. He had a terrible headache. He was sore all over. In the morning, he was taken to the hospital. Thankfully, the doctors didn't find anything wrong. But the team didn't want to take any chances, so Pelé didn't play soccer for three weeks. When Pelé rejoined Santos, he thought he'd be rusty. But he didn't miss a beat. He kept scoring, and the team kept winning. On March 1, 1961, Pelé scored a goal some believe was his most spectacular.

During a game at the Maracanã, Pelé got the ball just outside the Santos penalty box. He quickly ran up the field. One by one, defenders tried to stop him. One by one, they failed. Pelé dribbled around them, past them, through them. No one could stop Pelé. His footwork was incredible! Finally, Pelé approached the other team's goal. There was just one player left—the goalkeeper. Pelé aimed and kicked. The ball rocketed into the net for a goal!

The São Paulo newspaper made a bronze plaque to honor the goal. They called it the "most beautiful goal" ever scored at the Maracanã. The plaque still hangs on the wall outside the stadium. The goal is now known as the "goal of the plaque." The goal of the plaque seemed to stir something inside Pelé. He'd always been a great goal scorer, but he started scoring at an incredible rate. He scored five goals in a game in Switzerland. In September 1961, he played six games and scored twenty-three goals. "I couldn't stop scoring," he said. The king had amazed even himself.

Pele is the greatest player in football history, and there would only be one Pelé in the world.

—RONALDO, BRAZILIAN SOCCER STAR

With each goal, Pelé's fame grew. Two books were written about him. He starred in a film about his life. One day, he got a call from an Italian man. The man worked for Inter Milan, a famous Italian team. He offered Pelé a million dollars to play for Inter Milan. Pelé could hardly believe it! This was more money than he'd ever dreamed of making. But he didn't want to leave Brazil. He didn't want to leave his family and Rose, and so he turned down the offer.

The Brazilian government found out about the offer. To keep Pelé from moving to another country, the government declared him a national treasure. That meant Pelé couldn't sign with a team outside of Brazil. There was no doubting it now. The skinny kid from Bauru was a worldwide sensation. But Pelé didn't feel any different. He was still his happy, fun-loving self. And besides, he had something bigger on his mind. The World Cup was just around the corner.

Chapter | Six

Bittersweet Victory

Chile was host of the 1962 World Cup. As defending World Cup champs, Brazil was favored to win the title again. Many of the same men from 1958 were on the 1962 team. At twenty-one years old, Pelé was the youngest starting player. Since Brazil had won the World Cup in 1958, it automatically qualified for the 1962 tournament. Other teams would have to play their way into the tournament.

Still, the Brazilians needed to stay fresh, so they scheduled four practice games. In the first game, Pelé and his teammates took on Portugal. Brazil won. But afterward, Pelé was worried. He felt pain in his groin. He didn't want to complain, so he didn't tell the team doctor. The next day, he went to practice and the pain was still there. In the next three games, Pelé scored four goals. Two were game winners. He certainly didn't play like he was hurt. But he was. And it was getting worse. Pelé was scared to see the doctor, but he knew he had no choice. The doctor wasn't much help. He told Pelé that if he was hurt, he shouldn't practice. But Pelé knew that if he didn't practice, he wouldn't play. So he kept practicing.

---

66 *One thing I always try to do when I'm in public is to remain friendly and polite when people come up to me to say hello. I know how good it is to be with them— after all, I have idols of my own.* 99

—PELÉ

Finally, in May, the Brazilian team headed to the tournament. The team flew over the Andes Mountains and into Chile. The flight was bumpy, and most of the players were scared. Not Pelé. He just sat calmly in his seat. "The others were going crazy, saying that I was crazy," Pelé said. "But what's the point in getting scared?"

Brazil played Mexico in its first game on May 30, 1962. Pelé scored a goal and had an assist in the 2–0 win. The goal was a thing of beauty. Pelé dribbled through four defenders, then blasted the ball past the Mexican keeper. But after the game, Pelé didn't feel well. As he left the field, he felt unusually tired. Pelé knew he should see the doctor. But he didn't want to be benched, so he kept quiet.

Pelé took the field against Czechoslovakia three days later. It was a big game for Brazil. They needed to win or tie if they wanted to stay in the tournament. Things were okay at the start of the game. Pelé's leg was holding up fine. Later in the first half, Pelé got the ball. He dribbled toward the Czech goal. Defenders came at him, but no one could stop him. It was like he had never been hurt at all!

When Pelé reached the penalty box, he shot. The ball hit the post—and bounced right back to him. This time, Pelé shot harder. An incredible pain shot through his leg. He fell to the ground. The doctor rushed to him, but there wasn't much he could do. They asked Pelé if he wanted to come out. Back then, teams weren't allowed substitutes. The coaches figured that eleven players were better than ten—even if one of them could hardly walk. Pelé knew he was seriously hurt. But he didn't want to let the team down. "I gritted my teeth and told the doctor I was okay to continue," he said. Pelé hobbled around the field the rest of the day. He could barely move, but he tried his best. Thankfully, the Czech players were kind. They could have tried to hurt him more, but they didn't. Pelé was thankful for the show of sportsmanship. "It was one of the finest things that happened to me in my entire career," he said.

Neither team could get anything going. The game ended in a 0–0 tie. Pelé and his teammates returned to their hotel. By now, Pelé could hardly walk. The team doctor was worried. He was sure Pelé wouldn't be able to play for the rest of the World Cup. But Pelé thought differently. He was young and strong! He just needed to rest. Pelé was sure he wouldn't miss any games.

The injury was treated day and night. Pelé kept the leg wrapped in hot towels. Garrincha, his close friend and teammate, offered support. "You're not going to abandon me, are you?" he asked Pelé. "You'll get over this and you'll be playing soon." Pelé hoped Garrincha was right. But the treatments didn't seem to help. Pelé was afraid the doctor was right after all.

The day before Brazil's next game, Pelé went to the doctor. He said he would take a shot of painkillers if it meant he could play. The doctor wouldn't allow it. "It might cripple you for life," he told Pelé. "I am not willing to risk that." The other players tried to cheer up Pelé. They told him not to worry. But how could he not? He loved playing soccer more than anything. And because of his injury, all he could do was lie around.

On June 6, 1962, Brazil beat Spain 2–1. Pelé watched the game on television. He was glad the team won. Amarildo, his replacement, was the star of the game, scoring both goals for Brazil. Pelé wondered if this kid would replace him as the team's star. Pelé had played in so many games in the past year. Nearly 100! He knew even the strongest person would break down under such strain. But why now, during the World Cup of all times?

Then, one morning, Pelé's leg felt better. Much better. For the first time in weeks, he had hope. He started practicing, but carefully. Pelé didn't want to risk making his leg worse. But it sure felt great to be back on the field. Pelé still wasn't ready when Brazil took on England in the quarterfinals. England thought that without Pelé, Brazil could be beat. They were wrong. Brazil won easily, 3–1. They'd face the host nation, Chile, in the semifinals. Pelé desperately wanted to play in the game.

He continued to practice, but the team decided he wasn't ready. So Pelé watched Brazil play Chile from the stands. If he couldn't help the team with his legs, maybe he could with his voice. He cheered them on to a 4–2 victory. The World Cup was down to just one more game. Everyone wondered if Pelé would play in the final against Czechoslovakia. And if he couldn't, did Brazil have a chance? There was no doubt in Pelé's mind. He would be on the field. After all, he'd been hurt playing against Czechoslovakia. It would be the perfect game for his comeback.

In the days leading up to the final, Pelé did everything he could to help his leg heal. He even took it easy at practice. One day, Pelé decided to work on corner kicks. He lined up and let it fly. He knew something was horribly wrong right away. "Never had I felt such pain," he thought. Pelé's heart sank. He knew he wouldn't play in the World Cup final. He began to cry. He couldn't believe it. So much hard work for nothing. "It seemed so unfair," he said later. "After turning up to games day in, day out, here I was sidelined before the second-biggest game of my life."

Pelé was terribly disappointed. But he wanted to support his team. He did everything he could to help. He took part in meetings and offered the others all the advice and encouragement he had. So, during the 1962 World Cup final, Pelé was a spectator. "It wasn't easy watching it all from the stands," he said. Brazil rolled to a 3–1 victory. After the game, the players went wild. Pelé joined in the celebration, but his heart wasn't completely in it. He was happy for his teammates. But he was also worried about his place on the team and his future as a player.

Back in Brazil it was one big party, with parades, dinners, banquets. But Pelé just wanted to go home. He'd never felt so low. He wondered if he'd ever be the player he was before the injury.

Chapter | Seven

Continuing to Shine

Even though Pelé was feeling down, he was determined not to give up. The Brazilian people helped him get through this difficult time. Everywhere he went, people offered encouragement. Pelé also drew strength from his family. He remembered the lessons he'd been taught as a boy. He had learned to be polite and kind and to be honest, responsible, and humble. Most important, he learned to work hard at everything he did. All this helped keep up Pelé's spirits.

Two months after his injury, a well-rested Pelé got a needed boost of confidence. In August 1962, Santos was playing in the Libertadores Cup in Argentina. The winner would be champion of South America. Santos made the finals, and Pelé scored two goals in a 3–0 win. Santos was the first Brazilian team ever to win the tournament. After the game, fans rushed on the field. They tore off all of Pelé's clothes—including his shorts!

45

STRANGE REQUESTS

As Pelé became more famous, he received more requests from fans. Some were stranger than others. A Brazilian taxi driver demanded that Pelé buy him a new car. Then a fan in England asked Pelé to come to his house to sign his wall. Pelé said he couldn't go. The next day, the man showed up with a piece of plaster. "You couldn't come to my wall, so I brought it to you," the man said.

Not long after this victory, Pelé again showed he hadn't lost the magic. Against Benfica, a Portuguese club, he scored two goals. The teams then played again—this time in Portugal. Pelé and his Santos teammates were surprised to see signs that read "Benfica: World Champions." Santos was ready to teach Benfica a lesson. Just minutes into the game, Pelé scored. Later, he scored again. He danced past five defenders before firing the ball into the net. Even the Benfica fans cheered!

In the second half, Pelé assisted on another goal. His performance was amazing. But he wasn't finished. Pelé was unstoppable. He scored two more goals, giving him four in the game. "It was a piece of soccer I'll never forget," he said. "After the disappointment of Chile, it was like starting a new life."

Back in Brazil, twenty-two-year-old Pelé was the most famous soccer player in the world. But he still didn't have his own home. He lived with a local family in Santos along with several of his teammates. Pelé was feeling good about soccer again. But being a world-famous player made things tough. Opponents singled him out. They thought if they could stop Pelé, they could beat Santos. Some got rough with Pelé and tried to make him angry. They thought that if they got Pelé mad, he wouldn't think about soccer. But Pelé didn't fall for their tricks. He was too smart for mind games.

Still, Pelé wasn't afraid to stand up for himself when the abuse went too far. During one game, a couple of opponents taunted him nonstop. Pelé ignored them. But they wouldn't quit—even after Pelé scored a goal. In fact, the goal only seemed to worsen the taunting. Late in the game, Santos was losing by one goal. Pelé was really hearing abuse from the two opponents. Then with just minutes left, Pelé scored a goal to tie the game. He ran into the net and grabbed the ball. He ran over to one of the opponents who'd been teasing him. Pelé handed the player the ball. "Here—it's a present from the king," Pelé said with a smile.

The countries of Brazil and Argentina have always been fierce rivals. And it's no different in soccer. Some of the toughest games Pelé played were against Argentinean teams. One was in the 1963 Libertadores Cup final in Buenos Aires, which is the capital of Argentina. The stadium was one of the scariest Pelé had ever played in. It was very loud, and the stands were very close to the field. The players felt like the fans were right on top of them.

In the game, Pelé was hounded from the start. He was pushed, bumped, shoved, and kicked. But Pelé soon showed them why he was called the "king." With just eight minutes left, Pelé got the ball. He raced past one defender. Two more came at him. But Pelé shot past them—and past the goalie. Santos had won! "The joy of scoring felt like nothing I'd experienced before. I was euphoric," said Pelé.

❝This is not our life/Everything here is a game/A passing thing/What matters is what I've done/And what I'll leave behind/Let it be an example/For those that come.❞

—FROM A POEM WRITTEN BY PELÉ

Santos's leaders wanted to take full advantage of Pelé's fame. More and more games were scheduled overseas. Pelé didn't mind. He enjoyed playing in Europe. The fans were friendly, and they knew their soccer. Pelé noticed that the European teams had improved a lot since he started playing.

Santos tried to improve too. To do so, they hired a man who would play a key role in Pelé's life.

Professor Julio Mazzei was hired in 1964 to help the team with its physical training. Santos was lucky to have Mazzei. He was a great teacher. He helped the players with everything, not just soccer. Pelé and Mazzei became very close. In fact, Pelé thought of him as a brother. With these good feelings, Pelé returned to the scene of one of his biggest disappointments. In 1962, he'd been hurt for most of the World Cup in Chile. Now, in January 1965, he was back in Chile to play Czechoslovakia—the same team he'd been playing when he was injured. Pelé was determined to show them that he was still one of the best in the world. He scored three goals in Santos's 6–4 win. A Chilean newspaper called it the "game of our dreams."

Pelé returned to Brazil. He was twenty-five years old, and he'd been dating Rose for seven years. They'd discussed getting married, but Rose always said it was too soon. But now, Pelé felt the time was right. He was making a good living. He finally had a house of his own. His big house was right on the beach. His mom, dad, brother, and sister lived with him. It seemed only right that Rose should live there too—as his wife. So Pelé asked Rose to marry him, and this time she said yes.

In early 1966, Pelé and Rose were married in a small wedding with just a few friends and family. The newlyweds honeymooned in Europe. They visited Germany, Switzerland, and Austria. In Italy, they met the pope, which was a dream come true for Rose. Finally, Pelé and Rose flew home to Brazil, happy but tired from their travels.

The happiness was spoiled when Pelé learned that he was almost out of money. He was also deeply in debt. Although Pelé was making good money by Brazilian standards, the amount was small compared to the huge salaries modern athletes earn. Pelé had looked for ways to make his money go further. Years before, he had hired a man named Pepe Gordo to help him manage and invest his money. Pelé found out Pepe had lost nearly all of the money, thanks to several bad investments. Pelé felt betrayed. There was no proof of any criminal wrongdoing by Gordo, so Pelé couldn't take legal action. But Pelé fired Gordo and decided he would watch over his own money from that day forward. With his finances in ruin, Pelé didn't think things could get much worse. He'd soon find out he was wrong.

Chapter Eight

The Disaster of '66

Pelé needed something to take his mind off his worries. The upcoming World Cup in England was just the thing. If Brazil could win, it would be the first team to win the cup three times in a row. But Pelé was concerned that the other players and coaches were stuck in the past. "Everyone was still talking about the titles Brazil had won in Sweden and Chile," Pelé said.

Pelé also felt the team managers were overly confident. They seemed to think Brazil had already won the tournament, and the games hadn't even started. Even the fans were caught up in the frenzy. "There wasn't a soul who was not touched by this exaggerated optimism," he said. Pelé grew more concerned as the day to leave for England drew closer. The team's planning wasn't being handled with the same care and humility, he believed. A bad feeling filled Pelé's heart.

The selection of players was also handled poorly. More than forty players were picked to try out for the team. Pelé thought that was far too many. Even worse, the players were divided into several teams instead of making up just one team. Pelé felt this was a mistake. How could the players get to know one another if they weren't playing together? Another problem was that the team didn't have a permanent home. Instead of training in one city, the team moved around, all over Brazil. Pelé felt all the traveling was a needless distraction. As the players boarded the plane for Europe, Pelé had a sinking feeling. He wondered if Brazil would even win a single game.

Pelé's doubts grew stronger as the Brazilians began their warm-up games. The team leaders were still trying to decide who the eleven starters would be. Different players played in each game. This made it difficult for the men to bond. And Pelé knew teams that weren't united usually didn't get very far—especially in the World Cup.

Things just kept getting worse. Brazil played Scotland in an exhibition game and managed to tie, 1–1. Pelé's teammate Servilio scored Brazil's goal. Pelé felt like he and Servilio played well together. But after the game, Servilio was dropped from the team. So was the goalkeeper. This confused Pelé. He was even more worried. Strangely, the other players didn't seem to care. To Pelé, they only thought about themselves and not the team. Finally, the exhibition matches were over. The Brazilians boarded a plane for England. Everyone felt the team's third World Cup in a row was locked up. Everyone except Pelé.

When the plane landed, the team took a bus to Liverpool, a city in northern England. The Brazilians stared out their windows in disbelief. The cars were driving on the wrong side of the road! The team later learned cars drive on the left side of the road in England. Everyone had a good laugh about it. For the first time, Pelé felt good about the team. But it wouldn't last.

The bus arrived at the hotel, and the Brazilians got settled. Pelé wanted to explore the city, but the team leaders didn't want the players to leave the hotel. Pelé understood, but he was disappointed. He also felt the team leaders didn't understand the younger players.

Liverpool was home to a famous rock band called the Beatles. Pelé found out that the Beatles were huge soccer fans. The band contacted the Brazilian team. They wanted to put on a tribute concert for the players. Pelé thought this was a great idea! It would help the team relax. But Brazil's team leaders said no.

Brazil's 1966 World Cup kicked off against Bulgaria on July 12. The eleven Brazilian starters had never been together on the same field before. It was crazy, Pelé thought. How could players who hadn't all played together be expected to win? Somehow

Brazil managed a 2–0 victory. Pelé scored on a banana kick in the first half. (A banana kick is when a player kicks the ball off center with the outside or inside of the foot. This causes the ball to curve.) Garrincha, Pelé's old friend, scored the second goal. It would be the last time the two would play together. Garrincha retired from international play after the 1966 World Cup.

A MUSICAL GAME

Music is an important part of Brazilian culture. Pelé loves to play the guitar. He has even written songs that have been recorded by several Brazilian stars. Pelé also believes music plays a key role in his style of soccer. "Without a doubt, the way Brazilians play soccer is connected with rhythm, melody, and beat," he says.

After the victory, Brazil's team leaders felt that their plan was coming together perfectly. But Pelé knew better. Yes, Brazil had a lot of good players. But good players didn't win the World Cup—great *teams* won the World Cup. And Brazil still lacked unity. The Bulgarians might have lost, but their effort took its toll. Pelé's legs were sore from the rough play. "They did everything they could to cripple me," he said. Pelé was also frustrated by the referees. He felt they did little to protect him and his teammates.

Concerned about their star player, the team leaders decided to keep Pelé out of the next game. Pelé thought this was a mistake. If Brazil beat Hungary, it would qualify for the second round. Then Pelé could rest in the first round's final game. But he didn't want to cause any trouble, so he didn't say anything.

Pelé knew Hungary, a European soccer power, would be difficult to beat. Brazil fell behind 1–0 early, then tied the score before halftime. If the game ended in a tie, Brazil would still qualify for the next round. But Hungary had other plans. Time after time, they attacked Brazil's disorganized defense. Hungary went ahead and never looked back, winning 3–1. Brazil was in unfamiliar territory. The two-time World Cup champions needed a miracle to make the second round.

Sixteen teams, divided into four groups, were in the 1966 World Cup. Each group had four teams. All the teams in a group played each other once. Those with the best record in each group moved into the second round. To win its group, Brazil would have to beat Portugal, a win that would create a tie for first place in the group. In case of a tie, the team with the most goals would move on. Brazil was far behind Portugal in goals scored, so Pelé and his teammates would have to outscore Portugal by several goals to win the group.

In the days before the game, Pelé's worry grew. He felt Brazil's team leaders were cracking under the pressure. Nobody knew who would be starting and who would be on the bench. Finally, Pelé learned he would start. He wasn't completely healthy, but it was now or never. Sadly, Pelé wasn't the only Brazilian who was hurting. Several other players were injured. One was Gilmar, the team's goalkeeper. Manga, his replacement, was young and new to the World Cup, and Pelé wondered if he could handle the stress.

From the start, the game was a disaster. After fourteen minutes, Brazil was down 1–0. After twenty-four minutes, it was 2–0, Portugal. Pelé had thought Bulgaria's players were rough, but Portugal's players were even more aggressive. One player, named Morais, hounded Pelé the entire game. At one point, Morais took Pelé down with a vicious tackle. Pelé looked to the referee for help, but the referee did nothing. Frustrated and in great pain, Pelé got up and kept playing.

Rildo, a defender, didn't often get a chance to score, but Pelé's twenty-four-year-old teammate gave Brazil some life in the second half by scoring the team's first goal. The score was now 2–1, but Portugal wouldn't be stopped. By the end of the game, Pelé was limping badly. Portugal scored again and won, 3–1. Brazil was out of the tournament. It seemed that their World Cup dominance was over.

Pelé was upset by the rough play he'd encountered in the World Cup. But he refused to use it as an excuse. "We played our best. We played our hearts out," he said. To make matters worse, the World Cup final was to be held in London's Wembley Stadium. Pelé had long dreamed of playing on that famous field, but that dream would have to wait.

Brazil's players and coaches boarded their plane for the long flight back home from Liverpool. In London, the players were told that the plane was delayed for mechanical repairs. Pelé learned later that the team leaders made the plane wait for different reasons. They wanted to arrive in Brazil in the middle of the night to avoid what might be an angry reception.

When the plane finally touched down in Rio, there was no crowd. The players were relieved. They were embarrassed and didn't want to face anyone. As he left the plane, Pelé thought about the past few weeks. The team had been poorly prepared, and the players were out of shape. Management didn't know what they were doing, and he was sick of being roughed up on the field while the referees did nothing. The more Pelé thought about it, the more frustrated he became. By the time he flew to São Paulo, Pelé had reached an important decision. He was never going to play in the World Cup again.

Chapter | Nine

Redemption

The 1966 World Cup had taken a lot out of Pelé—both physically and psychologically. He was disappointed in how soccer had changed over the years. The players were more violent, and the referees were weaker. Pele wondered what had become of good sportsmanship. Still, many didn't believe Pelé when he said he'd never play in the World Cup again. They didn't know just how tough the 1966 contest had been on Pelé. He'd scored fewer goals that year than in any previous year. And on top of that, he was almost always banged up and hurt.

But not everything was doom and gloom. In 1966, Pelé made his first trip to New York City. Santos was playing in a tournament that included Benfica. This team was made up of players who had been on the Portuguese team that had knocked Brazil out of the 1966 World Cup. Pelé and his teammates wanted revenge. "We were desperate to show them what we could do," Pelé said.

Edson Arantes do Nascimento was given the nickname Pelé when he was young. In this photo, he was sixteen years old.

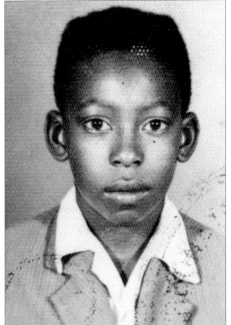

Pelé *(second from left)* scores a goal during the 1958 World Cup final to help lead Brazil past Sweden.

Pelé does a bicycle kick during a game in the 1960s.

Pelé *(center)* stands with his father, Dondinho, and mother, Celeste, in 1965.

Pelé celebrates his 1,000th goal on November 19, 1969.

Pelé heads the ball past Italy's defender Tarcisio Burgnich and into the goal during the 1970 World Cup finals in Mexico on June 21, 1970.

Pelé (10) takes in the moment after finishing his last match for the Brazil national team on July 18, 1971.

Pelé runs to the ball during the 1977 North American Soccer League Championship. Pelé's Cosmos defeated the Seattle Sounders 2–1.

Pelé waves an American and a Brazilian flag while being carried from the field after his final professional game on October 1, 1977. The Cosmos played his old Brazilian club team, Santos.

With a Brazilian flag around his shoulders, Pelé celebrates the announcement that Rio de Janeiro will host the 2016 Summer Olympic Games.

Playing against Benfica, Pelé saw something that would give him hope for soccer in the United States, where soccer wasn't a popular sport. But on that day, Pelé said the crowd was one of the most excited that he could remember.

Santos didn't disappoint the Americans, rolling to a 4–0 win. Pelé scored one of the goals. At one point, the fans were so excited that they stormed the field. Police had to restore order before the game could resume. The win didn't make up for the World Cup loss, of course, but it still felt good. The victory was a nice way to end what had been a difficult year.

The following year started out on a high note. On January 13, 1967, Pelé and Rose welcomed their first child into the world, Kelly Cristina. Before Kelly's birth, Pelé had struggled to find the enthusiasm for soccer that he had once had. He wondered how much longer he would continue to play. But becoming a father reignited his passion. Kelly helped Pelé look at life in a new way. Playing with his daughter cheered him up. "It was impossible not to shrug off the pressures when I was around her," he said. "And she really helped me rediscover my love of the game."

Another important event in Pelé's life came a few months after Kelly's birth. For the first time, he and Santos traveled to southern Africa. It would forever change Pelé's view of the world. Everywhere Santos went, huge crowds greeted the team. "Everyone in Africa, it seemed, wanted to see us, touch us, almost as if they wanted to make sure we were real," he said. This touched Pelé deeply. Pelé's ancestors were Africans who'd been brought to Brazil as slaves. His grandparents were the first in the family to be born free. As he traveled through Africa, Pelé could see what his success meant to the people there. "To these people, who had little possibility of ever escaping poverty, I somehow represented a ray of hope, however faint."

A reporter once asked Pelé if there was anyone he wished he'd met during his travels. "Of all the people I've met, I was struck by Martin Luther King. And Nelson Mandela," Pelé said. "But the one I did not have the opportunity to talk with was Gandhi. I am sorry I did not meet him."

As Pelé left Africa, he thought about what he had seen and learned there. He felt he would carry the memory with him the rest of his life. The disappointments of 1966 were fading. His experiences in Africa and family life at home brought Pelé a happiness that he'd never known.

By 1968, Santos was back in top form. The team entered five major competitions and won all of them. They continued to travel the world, making new fans everywhere they went. Pelé became even more famous. He filmed television commercials promoting bicycles, shoes, and his own brand of coffee. Pelé even appeared on a soap opera!

At twenty-eight years old, Pelé was enjoying life more than ever. Pelé's life was good, but a little crazy. His schedule was demanding, and even things on the field got wild sometimes. During a game in Colombia, something happened that Pelé was sure had never happened before. After a controversial goal went against Santos, Pelé's teammate Lima argued with the referee. Lima was kicked out of the game. Pelé was angry and he let the referee know it, so he was kicked out as well.

Though Pelé was on the visiting team, he was the one the fans wanted to see. When they learned Pelé had been sent off, they went wild. They showered the field with garbage. Police went onto the field to protect the referee. "Pelé! Pelé!" the crowd roared. Officials knew they had to do something to calm the crowd. So they decided to kick the referee out of the game and let Pelé back in!

In 1969, Santos returned to Africa. Things were different this time, however. The team was scheduled to play exhibition games against teams in the Republic of the Congo and Nigeria. In Congo, Pelé and his teammates were shocked to see tanks and soldiers with guns in the streets. Nigeria was in the middle of a civil war, and the players hesitated to go there. The team's manager told the players not to worry. "They'll stop the war," the manager said. "It won't be a problem." Amazingly, he was right. Both sides agreed to a two-day cease-fire just so everyone could see the great Pelé!

 Pelé played in eighty-eight countries during his career. He met two popes, five emperors, ten kings, and more than one hundred other heads of state.

Back home in Brazil, Pelé continued his strong play. He starred for both Santos and Brazil's national team. He had a game nearly every day of the week. With each goal he scored, Pelé grew closer to a remarkable feat. No one had ever scored 1,000 goals, and the milestone was in his reach. In October, he was just 11 goals away from the magical number. Four goals in one game in October got him even closer. Excitement and anticipation grew, and so did the pressure. Pelé's thousandth goal was all anyone wanted to talk about, and he was growing tired of all the talk. He just wanted the chase for 1,000 goals to be over.

The attention from the fans and the media became more and more frenzied. After a goal against Santa Cruz on November 12, Pelé was just two goals away and reporters were going nuts.

The pressure began to get worse. The next game was two days later in the eastern Brazilian city of João Pessoa against Botafogo. Santos was already winning 2–0 when one of Pelé's teammates was fouled in the penalty box. Normally, Carlos Alberto took penalty shots for Santos. But this time, he refused. Alberto put his arm around Pelé. The two players looked up at the crowd. Alberto told Pelé he *had* to take the shot. Alberto pointed at the cheering fans and said they'd never let the players off the field if Pelé didn't take the kick. Alberto was right, so Pelé put the ball down, charged, and kicked. That was goal number 999.

But fans who hoped to see Pelé's historic goal had their hopes dashed. Later in the game, Santos's goalkeeper collapsed. He rolled around, seemingly in great pain. He was helped off the field by the team doctor. Since no substitutions were allowed, someone already on the field had to take over in goal. Though he was rarely called on to serve as such, Pelé was the backup goalie. He spent the rest of the game trying to stop goals rather than scoring them.

The next game was against Bahia, a team named after the eastern Brazilian state. People were excited at their chance to see history. They packed the stadium, waving flags and banging drums. The cheering never stopped. But Pelé wasn't feeling very excited. He was tired of all the attention. He couldn't wait to score number 1,000. He wanted to put it behind him once and for all. "I had long wished the thousandth goal was over and done with, but never as much as on this day," Pelé said. "I had a sudden cold feeling that I was doomed to go for years and years without scoring another goal."

He almost got his goal early in the game. But his shot hit the crossbar and bounced away. Later, he got another chance. Controlling the ball near the penalty box, Pelé turned and got past a defender. The goalkeeper ran out, but Pelé dribbled past him. The net was open! Pelé kicked the ball. He was sure this was goal number 1,000! Suddenly, a defender appeared. At the last moment, he kicked the ball away. The crowd booed. Pelé thought this was strange. Home fans booing their own player! Apparently, seeing a Pelé goal was more important than their team winning the game. Pelé ran back up the field, shaking his head at his bad luck. He finished the game without scoring a single goal.

Santos's next game was at the Maracanã three days later against Vasco. The anticipation was becoming unbearable. The world's largest stadium was filled with screaming fans. They were all there to see one thing—Pelé's thousandth goal. But Vasco didn't want to be the team that gave it up. They teased Pelé. "Not today," they said. And so the Vasco players did everything they could to stop Pelé. One player even headed the ball into his own goal to prevent Pelé from scoring. Pelé couldn't believe it!

Twice Pelé came achingly close to scoring. Once, he

chipped the ball over a crowd of players. The ball sailed toward the upper left corner of the goal. But the Vasco goalie leaped and punched the ball over the crossbar. Later, Pelé got close to the goal and shot. The ball bounced off a defender and came back to Pelé. Pelé shot again. This time the ball hit the crossbar. The crowd groaned. Pelé couldn't believe his bad luck!

But Pelé got another chance at history. Late in the game, he made a run toward the Vasco goal. A teammate made a perfect pass between two defenders. But before he could shoot, Pelé was tripped from behind. The referee blew his whistle. Santos was awarded a penalty shot. This time, there was no question who'd take it. "A penalty kick certainly wasn't the way I'd hoped to make my thousandth goal," Pelé said. "But at that point, I would have taken it any way I could, just to get it over with."

Pelé put the ball down and backed up. "For the first time, I felt nervous," he said. "I had never felt a responsibility like this before. I was shaking. I was on my own now." Pelé ran toward the ball. He felt like he was running in slow motion. Suddenly, a bad memory flashed through his mind. He remembered the penalty kick he'd missed in the junior game years before—the one that almost made him quit.

But Pelé pushed the thought from his mind. He ran to the ball and kicked. The ball rocketed toward the lower right corner of the goal. The goalie dove . . . but the ball went past him and into the net. At last, Pelé had scored goal number 1,000! He ran into the net and grabbed the ball. Then he kissed it! The crowd went wild. Fireworks went off. Pelé felt a great sense of relief. At last, the quest was over.

Fans ran onto the field. Journalists surrounded Pelé and stuck microphones in his face. He dedicated the goal to the children of Brazil and began to cry. The players lifted Pelé onto their shoulders and carried him around the field. Twenty minutes later, the game started again. But not many cared. Everyone had already seen what they had come to see.

At last the pressure was off, and Pelé could relax. He found his mind drifting to the World Cup, which was less than a year away. Just thinking about it stirred something inside him. After the disappointment of the 1966 World Cup, Pelé had vowed never to play in the tournament again. But that was three years ago. Time had healed his wounds. And besides, he didn't want his international career to have ended on a losing note. It didn't take Pelé long to reach an important decision—he would play for Brazil in the 1970 World Cup.

Chapter | Ten

The Dream Team

There was another reason Pelé wanted to play in the 1970 World Cup. Of the three World Cups he'd participated in, he'd never played in every game. In 1970, Pelé wanted to play in every game of the World Cup. He felt that he had something to prove and that Brazil's team leaders had learned their lesson from the 1966 disaster. They were determined not to make the same mistakes. "There was more understanding of the challenge ahead," Pelé believed.

Mexico was to host the 1970 World Cup. Pelé looked forward to playing there because the fans always treated him with respect. In fact, when Santos played Guadalajara, almost the whole city took the day off. The posters on every street corner made it clear who the Mexican fans supported. "No work today—we're off to see Pelé," the signs read. Other teams didn't feel the same way about going to Mexico. They complained about the heat and the elevation. But Pelé didn't complain. To him, soccer was soccer—no matter where you played it.

> ❝*Pelé spent twenty-two years playing soccer, and in that time, he's done more for goodwill and friendship than all of the ambassadors ever appointed.*❞
>
> —J. B. PINHEIRO, FORMER BRAZILIAN AMBASSADOR
> TO THE UNITED NATIONS

In 1969, things were going great for Pelé and the Brazilian team. But then the team's coach made some nasty comments about some of the Brazilian players, including Pelé. The coach told a reporter that Pelé would be kept off the team because of bad eyesight. Pelé couldn't believe it! True, he was a little near-sighted, but not nearly bad enough to keep him from playing. Pelé's teammates brushed off the coach's words. "Pelé is the player in whom we trust," Carlos Alberto said. Pelé found the best way to deal with the situation was with humor. He told people he would have 2,000 goals, not 1,000, if his eyesight was better!

The team management fired the coach and hired someone who was familiar to Pelé. Zagallo had been Pelé's teammate on the 1958 and 1962 World Cup teams. As a coach, Zagallo always listened to his players, and Pelé respected that.

Brazil won all six of its qualifying games. Pelé was on fire, scoring six goals in the six games. The team had spent more than a year playing together. Every player knew what to expect from everyone else. The situation was a far cry from the 1966 team. "We understood each other perfectly," Pelé said. "I think that is what gave us a great advantage."

Three weeks before the World Cup tournament began, the Brazilian team went to Mexico. They started off early because team leaders wanted the players to get used to the heat and elevation. At first, the conditions were tough to train in, but as time passed, the team got used to them.

For Brazil's national team, nothing was left to chance. Even the uniforms had some fancy new touches. Shirt collars were designed to not soak up sweat so players weren't weighed down by wet uniforms. Each player also had his uniform perfectly fitted. Some found this silly, but not Pelé. "Over 90 million people were counting on us to bring the trophy home," he said. Brazil would take any advantage it could get! The three weeks in Mexico brought the team closer together. "We lived as a family. We all got along," Pelé said. "With this, how could we fail?"

On June 3, 1970, Brazil began its quest for a third World Cup in a game against Czechoslovakia. More than 50,000 fans braved the oppressive heat to watch. Brazil's bad memories of 1966 returned when the Czechs took an early 1–0 lead. Before the World Cup, some reporters had said that Brazil was all offense, no defense. The Czech coach even said Pelé was washed up. After the goal by Czechoslovakia, some wondered if they were right. But Pelé and his teammates never panicked. They knew their team was good enough to come back. Ten minutes after the Czechs' first goal, Brazil tied the game on a free kick by Rivelino. Then came one of those moments that made Pelé a superstar.

Pelé had the ball near the center of the field. The Czech defense moved back, expecting Pelé to make a charge. Pelé looked up and noticed the Czech goalkeeper had moved forward, away from the goal. To the surprise of everyone, Pelé took a shot. The ball sailed high, then down toward the net. The Czech goalie scrambled back, but he was too late. Luckily for him, the ball went just wide. The crowd was stunned. Even Pelé's missed shots were legendary!

In the second half, Pelé got another chance to score. He trapped a pass with his chest, then volleyed the ball into the net. Two goals by Jairzinho capped off Brazil's 4–1 win. The victory was a great start, but the team didn't have much time to celebrate. Their next opponent was England, one of the top teams in soccer and the defending champion. They'd be one of the toughest teams Brazil would face in the World Cup.

Almost 70,000 fans filled Jalisco Stadium in Guadalajara to watch Brazil battle England. The noontime sun was blazing hot, which was to Brazil's advantage. The English climate is cloudy and cool, but Brazilians are used to playing in the heat. Still, Pelé wasn't about to get overconfident. "If they managed to score against us, I was afraid that Brazil might never reach the quarterfinals," he said. Just ten minutes into the game, Pelé was involved in one of the World Cup's most famous plays. He rushed toward the goal as Jairzinho made a perfect cross from the right goal line. Pelé leaped and headed the ball perfectly toward the lower corner of the goal. "As I watched the ball spin towards the net, I knew it was a goal," he said. But Gordon Banks, the English goalkeeper, thought differently. Banks dove and somehow managed to punch the ball up and over the crossbar. Pelé stared at Banks in amazement. "It was a phenomenal save," Pelé said. "It was the save of the tournament." Even Felix, Brazil's goalkeeper, applauded!

Banks kept making great saves. But Pelé and his teammates were patient and didn't give up. They kept coming at England. Finally, Brazil broke through. Pelé made a perfect pass to Jairzinho, who scored. It was the only goal of the game. Brazil hung on for a 1–0 victory.

Pelé scored twice in the team's final first-round game, against Romania. Brazil won, but Pelé wasn't happy with the

71

team's performance. He felt that everyone was overconfident and that the team was fortunate to beat the tough Romanian squad. Brazil's next game was a reunion of sorts. Pelé's old teammate Didi had become head coach of Peru's team. Didi had done an impressive job leading Peru, Pelé thought. But the Peruvians were no match for the Brazilians, who were looking for a strong game after the poor effort against Romania. They got their wish, winning 4–2. The game was Pelé's favorite of the World Cup so far. The style and pace were perfect. Both teams attacked the goal over and over. This was soccer at its best.

Brazil was headed to the semifinals. The team was anxious to find out who their opponent would be. So anxious, in fact, that they didn't shower right away. Instead they gathered around a radio in the locker room. Pelé and his teammates listened as Uruguay and the Soviet Union battled. Uruguay scored a late goal to win 1–0. So Brazil would play Uruguay in the 1970 World Cup semifinal. Finding out who their opponent would be took Pelé back to 1950. Brazil had been favored to win the World Cup that year. It had the best team, and it was the host nation. But Uruguay beat Brazil at the Maracanã in a loss that shocked Brazilian fans—including a nine-year-old Pelé. He had been so upset he'd cried himself to sleep.

The 1970 final was Pelé's chance to avenge that devastating loss. His teammates felt the same way. In fact, they felt beating Uruguay was almost more important than winning the World Cup. "We could not afford to lose," Pelé said. "Or we would have trouble facing a single soul back in Brazil." Game day arrived at last. Brazil started out poorly, reminding Pelé of the World Cup game in 1950. "We were making all the same mistakes," he said. "Bad passes, weak defense, and we couldn't get through our opponents at all." Then Uruguay took a 1–0 lead. Here we go again, Pelé thought.

But Brazil kept fighting. Pelé nearly tied the game, but the Uruguay goalkeeper made a fantastic save. Later, Pelé had the ball in the penalty box. Before he could shoot, he was knocked over. The Uruguayan defender also stepped on Pelé's ankle. Pelé looked up at the referee. Surely that was a penalty! But the ref did nothing. Frustrated, Pelé got up and kept playing.

Later in the match, Pelé was dribbling up the field when he saw the same Uruguayan player who'd knocked him down. The defender was coming in fast, from behind. Pelé knew he had to protect himself. Just as the Uruguayan was about to make a diving tackle, Pelé hit him in the head with his elbow. This time the referee blew his whistle. But the penalty was on the Uruguayan player. Pelé didn't like having to hit another player. It was something he always tried to avoid. But there were times when he had to defend himself. He was proud that he'd never been kicked out of a game for fouling someone.

The game was nothing like the semifinal against Peru. After Uruguay scored, the exciting, offensive style of play stopped. Uruguay pulled back every player but one to play defense. The Uruguayans were winning, and they had no interest in scoring more goals. They just wanted to keep Brazil from scoring. But the Brazilians wouldn't be stopped. They wanted to win this game badly. Near the end of the first half, they finally broke through to score the tying goal.

The tying goal was just what Brazil needed. Once the game was tied, everyone relaxed. In the second half, Brazil came alive. "We took control of the game, playing quick, smart soccer," Pelé said. Jairzinho and Rivelino scored to put Brazil up 3–1. As time ticked away, Brazil seemed likely to win. But Pelé had one more trick up his sleeve.

In the final minutes, a teammate sent a pass into Uruguay's penalty box. Pelé ran toward the ball, but so did the Uruguayan goalie. Just before the two met, Pelé darted left, around the goalkeeper. The ball, however, was on the right. Instead of following the ball, the goalie dove for Pelé. Both the ball and Pelé went past the goalkeeper, but on opposite sides! Pelé raced to the ball. He was off balance, but he managed to get off a shot. The ball sailed just wide of the goal. "Now we know, if we ever doubted it before, why they call this man the king, why he's known as the greatest soccer player in the world," an English television broadcaster said. Pelé smiled. He hadn't scored, but once again he'd made a play that would go down in soccer history!

When the final whistle blew, Brazil had won its revenge. "We were a better team than the Uruguayans, just as we were in 1950," Pelé said. "The difference now was that, twenty years on, it was the better team that won." Brazil was just one win from making history, but so was its opponent. Italy had also won two World Cups. Whoever won this game would be the first to have three World Cup trophies.

The game was a contrast in styles. Italy was known for its defense. Brazil was known for its offense. The match captured imaginations around the world. Nearly one billion people watched the game on television, and for the first time the World Cup was televised in color. Inside Azteca Stadium in Mexico City, 100,000 fans braved the heat to watch the two teams battle for the championship.

The Italians had a great defense. But to beat Brazil they would have to find a way to score. Unfortunately for Italy, Pelé and his teammates were at the top of their game. "It was one of my best games in a Brazil uniform," Pelé would later say. Just twenty minutes into the game, Pelé cracked the Italian defense. Rivelino sent a high cross into the box. Pelé jumped and seemed to hang in the air. "He was up there, waiting—it was an incredible thing," Rivelino said. Defender Tarcisio Burgnich was also amazed. "We jumped together, then I came down, but Pelé stayed up there," Burgnich said. The ball sailed toward Pelé, and he headed it into the net. Italy's goalkeeper never had a chance. "I told myself before the game that Pelé was made of skin and bones just like everyone else," Burgnich said. "I was wrong."

USING HIS HEAD

Pelé's goal in the 1970 World Cup final is one of his favorites—thanks to his dad. "I have a special feeling for that goal because I scored it with my head. My father was a soccer player and once scored five goals in a game, all with his head. That was one record I was never able to break."

Brazil was up 1–0. But the Brazilians wanted more. Italy's defense stiffened. Brazil continued to attack, but the team couldn't break through for another goal. Then disaster struck. Brazil's Clodoaldo made a bad pass near his team's goal. Italy made him pay for the mistake by scoring a goal to tie the game, 1–1. Italy's strategy seemed to be working. Then with the first half winding down, Pelé broke through into open space. He lined up to shoot. The ball went into the net for a goal—or so

Pelé thought. Right before his shot, the whistle had blown for halftime. Pelé couldn't believe his luck.

Fans wondered if the Italians would have the advantage in the second half. After all, they were still tied with the mighty Brazilians. Perhaps Brazil would get frustrated and panic. But the Brazilians had other plans. They played with patience, calmly mounting attacks on the Italian goal. Finally, Gerson rocked a long shot into the net. Brazil led 2–1. Just five minutes later, Jairzinho added another goal. Pelé and his teammates knew they were in control. The Italian team's defense had let them down, and their offense wasn't strong enough to come back. The Brazilians relaxed. The World Cup was theirs!

This was Pelé's final World Cup match. He'd played brilliantly, and just before the game ended he showed why he was considered the greatest player in the world. He made a perfect pass to Carlos Alberto, who blasted the ball into the net for a 4–1 lead. Soon after, the referee blew his whistle. Brazil had won its third World Cup! The fans went crazy. People stormed the field, tearing the shirts—and even shorts—from the players for souvenirs. "I had to make sure to take my shirt off myself so my head didn't go with it!" Pelé said. A crowd lifted Pelé to its shoulders and carried him around the stadium. At last, the Brazilians made their way into the locker room to celebrate.

Pelé snuck off to the shower for a moment of quiet. He thought of all he'd gone through to reach this moment. He thought of his family and how they'd supported him. Then he rejoined his teammates as they went back onto the field to collect their trophy. The moment was emotional for everyone. "The intensity as Carlos Alberto lifted the trophy above his head, tears of joy in his eyes, was like nothing I had ever known," Pelé said. Pelé's World Cup career was over. It was an amazing journey. He'd reached one of his most important goals by playing in every game of the 1970 World Cup. "I felt as though I had achieved everything I had set out to achieve," he said. As he thought back over all the games, Pelé had no regrets. Well, *almost* none. He would have really loved to have scored a goal on a bicycle kick!

The team flew home for the usual round of receptions and special dinners. But some people were upset with Pelé. They couldn't understand how a player who was still on top of his game wouldn't play the World Cup ever again. But Pelé had made up his mind, and he knew he'd made the right decision. "I had helped Brazil win three World Cups. I had done my part," Pelé said. "I thought it was time the younger guys got a chance."

Pelé enjoyed celebrating with his fellow Brazilians, but he was worn out. His mind was on his wife, who was pregnant and wanted Pelé to come home. Pelé flew to be by her side. On

August 27, 1970, Rose gave birth to a boy, Edinho. Pelé was very happy and began to think more about his future. He wondered what he would do when he was done playing soccer. He didn't want to be just a soccer player. He wanted to learn, to educate himself. And he wanted to be a good example to his children. Pelé felt he hadn't taken school seriously when he was younger. His education had ended after he finished junior high school at the age of fourteen, when he went to work to help the family. So after discussing the idea with Rose, Pelé decided to go back to school. He had to pass were several rounds of tests before he could go to college. When Pelé wasn't playing soccer, he was studying. The studying wasn't easy, but bit by bit he moved toward making his dream come true.

Before one test, Pelé was very nervous. His old friend Professor Julio Mazzei was with him. "Relax, Pelé. Don't be nervous," Mazzei said. "You've worked hard and studied hard. You're completely prepared. Don't think of failing and you'll have no trouble." Pelé calmed down and passed the test. Finally, Pelé was accepted at the university in Santos. He earned a degree in physical education by day and played soccer by night. When he graduated, Pelé felt very proud. He'd worked hard and made another dream come true.

In 1971, Pelé decided to retire from the national team for good. He wanted to spend more time with his family. He remembered something his father had once told him. "You should stop when you are at your best, because that is how you will be remembered." One thing was certain—Pelé was at his best. He'd won three World Cups and scored more than a thousand goals. Brazil played two games to bid their star good-bye. The first was against Austria in São Paulo. Pelé only played in the first half, but he scored his final goal as a member of the national team. It was his seventy-seventh goal wearing Brazil's yellow jersey—a team record.

The second and final game was held in the Maracanã. More than 180,000 people filled the seats. Brazil and Yugoslavia tied 2–2, but no one cared who won or lost. They just wanted to watch the king one last time. Again, Pelé only played in the first half. He was disappointed with his play. "It was not the best game of my career," he said. "I was too emotionally involved, knowing I would never again wear the yellow and green colors of Brazil." When the game ended, the fans started chanting, "Stay! Stay!" Pelé ran around the stadium with tears in his eyes. "I can never forget the send-off I received from the loving crowd," he said.

While his career with the national team was over, Pelé was still a Santos player. In 1972, the team toured the world. Pelé played his thousandth game for Santos in Suriname, South America. All the years and all the games were catching up with him. He was tired of the constant travel and wanted to be at home with his wife and kids. Still, Pelé had a hard time letting go. He stayed on until

1974, when he decided to retire from Santos. The team's leader tried to convince him to stay, but Pelé had made up his mind.

Pelé's last game for Santos was against another São Paulo team, Ponte Preta. Nothing out of the ordinary happened until twenty minutes into the game, when Pelé caught a pass—with his hands! The other players stopped. The crowd went silent. Everyone was looking at Pelé. He ran to the center circle and dropped to his knees. He lifted his arms and turned to face each corner of the stadium. Tears ran down his face as he saluted the crowd. The fans rose to their feet. The cheers got louder and louder. Finally, Pelé stood up. It was too much. He couldn't bear to be on the field any longer. He ran into the locker room believing that, at thirty-three, he had played his last game.

 Pelé retired with 1,281 goals. He averaged one goal for every international game he played. He scored five goals in a game six times, four goals thirty times, and three goals ninety times.

As Pelé turned to his life outside of soccer, he realized he missed the game. But he didn't miss the travel and year-round schedule. He remembered a man he'd met in Jamaica a few years earlier. The man was named Clive Toye. Toye ran a professional soccer team in New York and had offered Pelé a contract to play for his team. Pelé had turned him down. But after Pelé's last game, Toye called again. The offer was still on the table. Pelé began to think about accepting. He wanted to make sure it was the right decision.

In 1973, Pelé started the International Youth Football Program, a series of soccer workshops for children around the world. The workshops were held every year for six years. "It turned out to be one of the best things I ever got involved with," Pelé said.

Pelé talked to Rose and Julio Mazzei. They listed all the reasons Pelé should play in the United States. Next to that list, they wrote down the reasons he shouldn't. When they were done writing, one thing was clear—Pelé would soon have a new home. "I would go to New York, and bring a little samba to the Big Apple."

82

Chapter Eleven

For the Love of the Game

At thirty-four years old, Pelé was excited to get back on the field. "When I retired, something inside me had died," Pelé said. "Playing soccer again would be like therapy." But the details of his contract took months to figure out. Finally, Pelé and the Cosmos came to an agreement. Soccer's brightest star was ready to take on his next challenge—helping Americans fall in love with soccer.

Pelé had been to the United States a few times with Santos. Rose had also visited New York City, and she loved it. "Rose liked the many advantages of New York: the ease of shopping, the theater, the museums—even the fact that the telephones worked, which was not always the case in South America," Pelé said.

There was one problem, however—Pelé knew very little English. But Professor Mazzei spoke the language perfectly. So Pelé arranged for the professor and his wife to also come to

New York. Being with such close friends would make the experience much easier for Pelé and Rose.

On June 11, 1975, the Cosmos introduced Pelé as their newest player. A press conference was held at the famous 21 Club in Manhattan. The room was packed with reporters and photographers. Everyone was thrilled that the Brazilian star would play in the United States, and Pelé did his best to answer everyone's questions. Professor Mazzei helped translate.

With the press obligations out of the way, Pelé set out to learn about his new team. He watched the Cosmos lose 1–0 to Vancouver on their home field. Then he traveled to Philadelphia, where the Cosmos lost again. Pelé could see that turning the team into a winner wouldn't be easy. "It was clear there was a lot of work to be done."

Finally, the moment everyone was waiting for arrived. Pelé's first game as a Cosmos player drew worldwide attention. The Cosmos beat Dallas in a game that Pelé hoped was a sign of things to come. But the rest of the 1975 season was a struggle for Pelé and the Cosmos. They finished with ten wins and twelve losses and didn't make the playoffs.

The level of play was far below what Pelé was used to in Brazil. Most of the other Cosmos players were in awe of him. "The biggest challenge for us was not stopping and watching him play," said Cosmos defenseman Werner Roth. Despite this,

Pelé was sure he could make his new team "shine like a jewel in a cabbage patch."

With the regular season over, the Cosmos flew to Europe and the Caribbean for some exhibition games. The team had its ups and downs, but the more the members played together, the better they became. When Pelé first joined the team, the other players were starstruck. They never dreamed they'd be on the same field as the great King Pelé. To his dismay, they would pass the ball to Pelé, then sit back and watch him. Pelé's teammates expected him to do everything. Pelé did his best to encourage them by passing the ball and telling them to shoot. He also complimented them when they made great plays. Pelé wanted the other players to feel that they were just as important as he was. As time went on, Pelé's teammates became more confident in their abilities. They no longer looked to Pelé to do everything. More and more, the Cosmos played like a team.

❝ When you're talking about Pelé, you're talking about history. ❞
— GIORGIO CHINAGLIA, NEW YORK COSMOS FORWARD

Off the field, things were going well. Rose found a beautiful apartment in Manhattan, and the family settled into their new home. Both children quickly learned English. Pelé's son, Edinho, was as sports crazy as his dad. But Edinho's favorite games were baseball and basketball, not soccer. In fact, when he was sixteen, Edinho won a prize at school. At the ceremony, the school principal called Pelé to the stage. He asked Pelé to present Edinho with the prize. Pelé agreed, assuming it was for soccer. "When I was up on the stage, I realized the prize was for best baseball player. It was a big surprise!"

Pelé was captivated by his new city—and his new city was captivated by him. He met famous people, such as singer Frank Sinatra and Mick Jagger of the Rolling Stones.

Pelé had a plan to build soccer's popularity in the United States. To Americans, Pelé was soccer. So he gave interview after interview. His picture appeared in newspapers across the country. To build interest in soccer, Pelé even went to baseball and football games. He hoped his presence would make sports fans curious about soccer.

Pelé was happy to see that his plan was working. Fans were coming to soccer games in record numbers. Pelé's fame continued to rise. Everywhere Pelé went, everyone knew who he was. U.S. interest in soccer was growing, just as Pelé had hoped.

In 1976, Pelé was ready for his first full season with the Cosmos. He was sure the team's progress would continue. Perhaps they could even make the playoffs this time. But some changes worried Pelé. An Englishman named Ken Furphy was the new coach. Pelé wasn't sure he was the right person for the team. Furphy liked a cautious, defensive style of play. This was a mistake, Pelé thought. "In my estimation, Furphy did not know how to motivate men. He was stubborn, for one thing." Things got worse when Furphy moved Pelé from forward to midfield. A forward's job is to score goals, and that's why the Cosmos had brought Pelé to New York.

The Cosmos won three of their first five games. It wasn't a terrible start, but Pelé had expected much more. At least the team no longer played in crumbling Downing Stadium. They now called Yankee Stadium home. Things brightened when New York signed Italian Giorgio Chinaglia. Pelé felt this was a smart move. The team desperately needed help on offense, and Chinaglia was a goal-scoring machine. "With Chinaglia joining us, I could see nothing but victory ahead," Pelé said. In his first game, Chinaglia made an immediate impact. He scored two goals. So did Pelé. The Cosmos won, 6–0. It looked like things were turning around. But the Cosmos only won half of their next eight games. The players grew more and more frustrated. To Pelé, clearly things were not working. The team needed a change.

Gordon Bradley was the Cosmos' coach when Pelé arrived in 1975. But in 1976, he took a different job with the team. As the season went on, the team's struggles worried him. Eventually, Furphy was fired and Bradley was again named coach. Pelé and his teammates were relieved. They won seven of their last eight games. An 8–2 win over Miami was a highlight. Chinaglia scored five goals, and Pelé added two of his own. The late charge moved the Cosmos into second place in the Northern Division. Even better, the Cosmos had made it to the playoffs!

Pelé knew the playoffs would be a good test for the Cosmos. Some of his teammates were used to pressure because they had played in Europe and South America. But Pelé wanted to see how the others would handle it. In the first round, every-one handled the pressure perfectly. Pelé scored a goal, and the Cosmos beat the Washington Diplomats 2–0. The win set up a meeting with the division-winning Tampa Bay Rowdies.

Rarely had there been more excitement about a U.S. soc-cer game. Tampa Bay was the best team in the North American Soccer League (NASL). The game was in Tampa Bay, where the Rowdies hadn't lost a game all season. But games like this were made for Pelé. He was eager to show U.S. fans what great soc-cer was all about.

A huge crowd of 40,000 fans showed up to watch. After Tampa Bay went up 1–0, Pelé scored a goal to tie the game. But the other Cosmos players struggled, and the Rowdies were just too tough. They scored two goals to pull away for a 3–1 win. Pelé walked off the field, sad but hopeful. "It was a disappointing end to a season of hard work. But at the same time, much progress was made—both at the Cosmos and for the sport in America."

The future of U.S. soccer never looked brighter. Attendance at games kept rising, and they were shown regularly on television. Kids all across the United States joined soccer leagues. Pelé had accomplished what he'd set out to do. He'd helped the United States fall in love with soccer!

For more than twenty years, Pelé had shared his passion for soccer with the world. His name was all over the record books. And while Pelé was just thirty-six years old, for a soccer player he was an old man. And so Pelé told the Cosmos that the 1977 season would be his last.

Pelé had nothing left to prove. But there was still one goal he wanted to reach. He wanted to win a league championship for New York's fans. He'd have one more chance to do it.

At the beginning of the season, securing the championship seemed impossible. The Cosmos were a mess. They had players from many different countries, and soccer was played differently around the world. The coaches had a difficult time finding a style that worked for everyone. Pelé was frustrated. Meanwhile, Fort Lauderdale was running away with the division.

Panic began to set in. Cosmos management started making changes. In May, they signed Franz Beckenbauer, captain of the World Cup champion West German team. In June, the Cosmos hired a new coach. But nothing seemed to work. Pelé's last season was slipping away when, miraculously, the Cosmos came alive. Not surprisingly, Pelé led the team's charge. He was playing better than he had in years, and he inspired his teammates to do the same. Management signed Pelé's old friend and teammate Carlos Alberto to strengthen the team's defense. Pelé was pleased. He knew Alberto would be a big help. Finally, everything seemed to be clicking.

New York once again had Cosmos fever. Fans packed Giants Stadium, the team's new home in New Jersey. The Cosmos gave them a show, winning their last eight home games. For the second year in a row, New York finished second in their division. But this year was different. The Cosmos were heading into the playoffs on a roll. And magic was in the air. Pelé could feel it.

In the first round, New York took on rival Tampa Bay. The Rowdies had knocked the Cosmos from the playoffs the year before. But this time, they were no match for the inspired Pelé and his teammates. The Cosmos beat Tampa Bay 3–0 in front of more than 55,000 fans.

Next up was division-winning Fort Lauderdale. A sellout crowd of 78,000 watched New York pound the Strikers, 8–3. Then New York beat Rochester in the semifinals. The win put the Cosmos in the Soccer Bowl, the NASL's championship game. Just one team—the Seattle Sounders—stood between the Cosmos and a title.

In August 1977, a crowd of 35,000 filled Civic Stadium in Portland, Oregon, to see if Pelé would go out on top. His teammates were determined to send him out a winner. "It's Pelé's final year, and we'd like him to leave the way he deserves to leave—as a champion," defender Werner Roth said. Things looked good for New York early. The Cosmos scored first. But the lead was short-lived. Seattle quickly tied the game. Then things went quiet. Neither team could put the ball in the net. New York mounted one last attack. Chinaglia scored on a header. At last, New York had the lead! But could they hold on? Pelé watched the clock. He just wanted the game to end. But time seemed to be going in slow motion.

Finally, the whistle blew. Pelé's final dream had come true. The Cosmos were champions! The Cosmos carried Pelé off the field as he held the NASL trophy high above his head. He was very proud of his teammates. They'd helped him bring the love of soccer to the United States. But they'd also helped him end his career as a winner. "We all felt responsible. It was Pelé's final game," said Cosmos striker Steve Hunt. "We wanted to do it for him."

Before Pelé could hang up his cleats for good, Cosmos management arranged a farewell tour. The team journeyed to Japan, China, India, and South America. Pelé had a wonderful time. At the end of the tour, the team returned to the United States for one last game at Giants Stadium. The opponent would be Pelé's beloved Santos.

---

66 *When Pelé is in Spain, the people there believe he is Spanish. When he is in England, they feel he is English. Russia, Yugoslavia, Turkey, France. It is all the same. Pelé is an international phenomenon.* 99

—PROFESSOR JULIO MAZZEI, PELÉ'S TRAINER

On a rainy October afternoon, 75,000 fans filled the stands to say good-bye to Pelé—and to share his farewell to the game he loved so much. "Even the sky was crying," said a Brazilian newspaper. Millions watched the game on television. And Pelé's parents sat in a special suite high above the field. The Cosmos had flown them in to see their son play for the last time.

In a special arrangement, Pelé played one half for each team. In the first half, wearing a Cosmos jersey, he displayed the old Pelé magic. He curved a free kick into the net from thirty yards out. The crowd went wild! The Cosmos swarmed Pelé in happiness. At halftime, Franz Beckenbauer led Pelé's dad onto the field. In the rain, Pelé gave Dondinho his number 10 Cosmos jersey. Father and son then shared an emotional hug.

In the second half, Pelé wore Santos's black-and-white striped jersey for the last time. Try as he might, there were no goals left in his magic feet. The final whistle blew, marking the end of an era. Rain poured down, but no one cared. "Pe-lé! Pe-lé!" the fans chanted. Tears flowed down Pelé's face. He was too overcome to wipe them away.

> ❝All the young people that you've turned on to this game will have nothing but deep feelings for a man named Pelé who, more than a great soccer player, is about elegance, about dignity, and we are very proud to have you in this country.❞
> —FRANK GIFFORD, INTERVIEWING PELÉ AFTER HIS FINAL GAME

Players from both teams ran up and hugged Pelé. Then they lifted him up and carried him around the field. He was given small U.S. and Brazilian flags and held one in each hand and waved to the fans, basking in their cheers. He couldn't bear to leave. He didn't want the day to end. But in his heart, he knew it was time to go. Pelé took one last look at the crowd, at the field, and at his fellow players. Then Pelé turned and ran to the locker room.

Epilogue

Citizen of the World

As a soccer player, Pelé made an incredible mark on the game. In fact, most people consider him the best of all time. But his impact has been just as important off the field. "Soccer had been my job for more than twenty years," he said. "And now it was time to use the fame it had given me in a positive way."

Pelé has used his fame to spread goodwill across the world. Helping children is one thing especially close to his heart. Pelé has worked tirelessly for the United Nations Children's Fund (UNICEF) to help children who suffer from hunger and disease. He has set up soccer camps for kids in several countries.

Pelé has made history in government too. In 1995, he was the first Afro-Brazilian man to become a government minister in Brazil. As Brazil's Minister of Sport from 1995 to 1998, Pelé helped promote the game—and the country—he loves so dearly. Former Brazilian president Fernando Henrique Cardoso called

Pelé "the symbol of Brazil, a man who has come up from his roots and triumphed." And Pelé believed he could use his worldwide fame to help "establish understandings between Brazil and other governments."

Soccer has played a huge role in Pelé's life. But unlike other players, he's never had the desire to be a coach. He also considered playing for Brazil in the 1986 World Cup, which would have made him both the youngest and the oldest player ever to have played in the World Cup. But in the end, Pelé decided against it.

Despite all his successes, Pelé hasn't been without his share of heartache. In 1978, Rose gave birth to the couple's third child, Jennifer. But Pelé was away on business at the time, and he missed the birth. Rose was very upset. She told Pelé that she could no longer handle him being away so much. The couple divorced—something Pelé called "one of the most difficult moments of my life."

Another dark moment came when Pelé and Rose's son, Edinho, was arrested for drug possession in 2005. "Those who know Edinho and lived with him could hardly imagine that this would happen," Pelé said. "Unfortunately, I was perhaps working too much and didn't notice. It's regrettable, because I've always fought intensely against drugs and I didn't notice this in my own house." Still, Pelé stuck by his son, and today Edinho is out of jail and a goalkeeper coach for his father's old team, Santos. "My father was my best representative while I was imprisoned, he looked out for what was best for me and saved me," Edinho said.

Pelé lost his own father when Dondinho died in 1996 at the age of 79. As always, Pelé saw love through the sadness. In the 1980s, he'd met Assíria Seixas Lemos through friends. Assíria is a famous gospel singer who has performed all over the world. The two grew close, and in 1994 Pelé married for a second time. Two years later, Assíria gave birth to twins, Joshua and Celeste, who was named in honor of Pelé's mother.

Pelé and Assíria spend their summers in New York and their winters in Brazil on a large ranch about one hundred miles southwest of São Paulo. Pelé calls the ranch his "haven" and cherishes his time there. "I'm in touch with nature," he says. "I sit in the shade of a tree and lose myself looking out to the fields, at the animals and the scrubland. I enjoy the peace and quiet tremendously." He still spends time with the three children he had with Rose. Through the good and bad times, Pelé has remained committed to one thing more than anything else—his family. "My family are the heart of everything. If it hadn't been for them, I wouldn't have achieved what I've achieved," he says.

As Pelé nears his seventieth birthday, he remains as vital a force in the world as he was fifty years ago as "El Rey," the king of soccer. Although he is one of the world's most famous athletes, Pelé has never forgotten his past. And even though his childhood was difficult, most of Pelé's memories are happy ones. "Sometimes I miss being the small boy who had never seen the sea," he says. "I miss the simplicity of life where happiness was playing soccer in a street full of friends."

OLYMPIC MILESTONE

In 2009, Pelé played a key role in bringing the 2016 Summer Olympic Games to Rio de Janeiro. He accompanied Brazilian president Luiz Inacio Lula da Silva to Copenhagen, Denmark, to help present Rio's case to the International Olympic Committee. Pelé told the committee that as an athlete, he had "one deep regret" in his life—not winning an Olympic medal. He joked that if the Olympics came to Rio, he'd finally get a chance to change that—at age 75! With Pelé's help, Rio was awarded the games.

Pelé says that sometime soon he will return to his ranch—for good. "I have achieved more than I could ever have imagined. I've had everything a man could hope for. It's been a thrilling life." But for now, Pelé will continue to do what he does best—spread the spirit of friendship and love across the world.

PERSONAL STATISTICS

Name:

Edson Arantes do Nascimento

Born:

October 23, 1940

Birthplace:

Três Corações, Minas Gerais, Brazil

Height:

5 feet 8 inches

Weight:

178 pounds

Position:

Forward

CAREER STATISTICS

Team	Games	Goals
Santos	1,117	1,094
Brazil (national team)	111	94
New York Cosmos	107	64
São Paulo (state team)	13	9
Brazilian Army	10	13
Santos/Vasco de Gama	4	6
NASL All-Stars	2	0
Athletes' Union (São Paulo)	2	0
All-Stars	1	0
Total	1,367	1,280

GLOSSARY

bicycle kick: a play in which a player kicks the ball in midair backward and over his or her own head, usually making contact above waist level

corner kick: a kick awarded to the offensive team when a member of the defensive team knocks the ball over the goal line. A corner kick is made from the corner of the field, where the goal line meets the sideline.

cross: a kick from one side of the field to the other

dribbling: controlling and moving the ball with the feet while running

forward: a player on a team responsible for most of a team's scoring. Forwards play upfield and take most of a team's shots.

free kick: a kick awarded to a player for a foul committed by the opposition. Opposing players must stand 10 yards away from the ball and cannot move until the ball is kicked.

goalkeeper (goalie): the player positioned directly in front of the goal who tries to prevent shots from getting into the net. The goalkeeper is the only player allowed to touch the ball with the hands and arms.

header: a play that uses the head to strike the ball

midfielder: a player in the middle of the field who supports both the forwards and fullbacks

NASL: the North American Soccer League. The professional soccer league in the United States from 1968 to 1985.

penalty box: a rectangular area in front of each goal. Goalkeepers can only use their hands when they are inside the penalty box. If a foul is committed in the box by the defending team, the offensive team is awarded a penalty kick.

penalty kick: a free kick that is awarded when a penalty occurs within the penalty box. Only the goalkeeper can defend a penalty kick.

save: a play in which the goalkeeper keeps the ball from going into the net

Seleção: the group of players from which the Brazilian national soccer team comes

tackle: a play in which a defender takes the ball from another player without tripping or fouling that player

trap: stopping the ball and controlling it using the body, legs, or feet

volley: a play in which a player kicks the ball when it is still in the air and before it touches the ground

SOURCES

1–2 Gentry Kirby, "Pele, King of Futbol," espn.go.com, n.d., http://espn.go.com/classic/biography/s/Pele.html (February 8, 2010).

3 Richard Deitsch, "Q+A with Pelé," sportsillustrated.cnn.com, August 1, 2005, http://sportsillustrated.cnn.com/vault/article/magazine/MAG1112178/index.htm (February 8, 2010).

4 James S. Haskins, *Pelé: A Biography* (New York: Doubleday, 1976), 39.

4 Harry Harris, *Pelé: His Life and Times* (New York: Welcome Rain, 2001), 14.

5 Ibid., 15.

5 Ibid., 16.

6 Pelé with Robert L. Fish, *My Life and the Beautiful Game* (New York: Doubleday, 1977), 67.

6–7 Harris, *Pelé: His Life and Times*, 19.

7 Ibid., 20.

7 Pelé, *My Life and the Beautiful Game*, 20.

8 Haskins, *Pelé: A Biography*, 59.

9 Harris, *Pelé: His Life and Times*, 23.

9 Haskins, *Pelé: A Biography*, 60.

10 Ibid., 65.

12 Ibid., 67.

12–13 Harris, *Pelé: His Life and Times*, 26.

13 Pelé with Orland Duarte and Alex Bellos. *Pelé: The Autobiography* (London: Simon & Schuster, 2006), 62.

13–14 Ibid., 63.

15 Harris, *Pelé: His Life and Times*, 27.

16 Pelé, *Pelé: The Autobiography*, 69.

17 Ibid., 70.

17 Ibid., 70.

17 Haskins, *Pelé: A Biography*, 70.

17 Pelé, *Pelé: The Autobiography*, 71.

18–19 Pelé, *My Life and the Beautiful Game*, 127.

19 Ibid., 127.

19 Pelé, *Pelé: The Autobiography*, 72.

19 Ibid., 73.

20 Ibid.

22 Ibid., 82.

24 Ibid., 303.

25 Ibid., 91.

25 Haskins, *Pelé: A Biography*, 84.

26 Pelé, *Pelé: The Autobiography*, 92.

27 Harris, *Pelé: His Life and Times*, 43.

27 Ibid., 43.

27 Ibid., 44.

30 Ibid., 48.

30 Pelé, *Pelé: The Autobiography*, 98.

31 Haskins, *Pelé: A Biography*, 49.

33 Pelé, *Pelé: The Autobiography*, 108.

33 Ibid., 81.

34 Pelé, *My Life and the Beautiful Game*, 158.

34 Pelé, *Pelé: The Autobiography*, 111.

35 Ibid., 112.

35 Ibid., 113.

35 Haskins, *Pelé: A Biography*, 95.

36 Pelé, *Pelé: The Autobiography*, 115.

38 Expertfootball.com, "Ronaldo," expertfootball.com, 2009, http://www.expertfootball.com/gossip/quotes.php?search=Ronaldo (February 8, 2010).

40 Pelé, *Pelé: The Autobiography*, 302.

40 Ibid., 123.

41 Ibid., 125.

41 Harris, *Pelé: His Life and Times*, 63.

42 Pelé, *Pelé: The Autobiography*, 126.

42 Harris, *Pelé: His Life and Times*, 63.

43 Pelé, *Pelé: The Autobiography*, 128.

43–44 Ibid., 128.

44 Ibid., 129.

46 Ibid., 302.

46 Ibid., 131.

47 Ibid., 136.

48 Ibid., 137.

48 Pelé, *My Life and the Beautiful Game*, v.

49 Pelé, *Pelé: The Autobiography*, 140.

51 Ibid., 145

51 Ibid.

54 Ibid., 244.

54 Harris, *Pelé: His Life and Times*, 80.

57 *Pelé, My Life and the Beautiful Game*, 198.

58–59 Pelé, *Pelé: The Autobiography*, 157.

59 Ibid., 159.

59–60 Ibid., 159.

60 Pelé, *My Life and the Beautiful*

60 Deitsch, "Q+A with Pelé."
62 Pelé, *Pelé: The Autobiography*, 166.
63–64 Pelé, *My Life and the Beautiful Game*, 216.
64 Pelé, *Pelé: The Autobiography*, 170.
65 Harris, *Pelé: His Life and Times*, 88.
65 Pelé, *Pelé: The Autobiography*, 170.
65 Ibid., 170.
67 Ibid., 174.
68 Hank Hersch, "SI Flashback: Soccer's Greatest Genius," sportsillustrated.cnn.com, June 1, 1999, http://sportsillustrated .cnn.com/centurys_best/ news/1999/05/19/siflashback _pele/ (February 8, 2010).
68 Harris, *Pelé: His Life and Times*, 97.
69 Pelé, *Pelé: The Autobiography*, 197.
69 Ibid., 177.
69 Ibid., 177.
71 Harris, *Pelé: His Life and Times*, 108.
71 Pelé, *Pelé: The Autobiography*, 181.
71 Ibid.
73 Harris, *Pelé: His Life and Times*, 117.
73 Pelé, *Pelé: The Autobiography*, 184.
74 Ibid., 185.
74 "Cybersoccer—1970 Brazil vs. Uruguay pt 20," Youtube.com, http://www.youtube.com/watch? v=r1SFxUdHMcQ&feature=related.
75 Pelé, *Pelé: The Autobiography*, 185.
75 Ibid., 186.
75 Garry Jenkins, *The Beautiful Team* (London: Simon & Schuster UK Ltd, 1998), 133.
76 Harris, *Pelé: His Life and Times*, 121.
76 Kirby, "Pele, King of Futbol."
76 Archana Srinivasan, Bio-Sporting Legends (Chennai: Sura Books., 2005), 44.
77 Pelé, *Pelé: The Autobiography*, 188.
78 Ibid., 189.
78 Haskins, *Pelé: A Biography*, 133.
79 Pelé, *My Life and the Beautiful Game*, 256.
80 Ibid., 199.
80 Ibid., 264.
80 Pelé, *Pelé: The Autobiography*, 200.

82 Ibid., 215.
82 Ibid., 205.
83 Ibid., 215.
83 Pelé, *My Life and the Beautiful Game*, 291.
84 Pelé, *Pelé: The Autobiography*, 221.
84 Gavin Newsham, "When Pelé and Cosmos Were Kings," guardian. co.uk, June 10, 2005, http://www. guardian.co.uk/football/2005/ jun/10/sport.comment (February 8, 2010).
85 Pelé, *My Life and the Beautiful Game*, 293.
85 *Once in a Lifetime*.
86 Pelé, *Pelé: The Autobiography*, 224.
87 Pelé, *My Life and the Beautiful Game*, 300.
87 Ibid., 301.
88–89 Pelé, *Pelé: The Autobiography*, 228.
91 *Once in a Lifetime*.
91 Ibid.
92 "Why Pelé Is a Worried Man," *New Straits Times*, January 3, 1986, 23.
92 Kirby, "Pele, King of Futbol."
93 *Once in a Lifetime*.
94 Pelé, *Pelé: The Autobiography*, 237.
94–95 Ibid., 259.
95 Ibid., 241.
95 "Pelé Admits Son's Drug, Gang Ties," Associated Press, June 8, 2005, http://www.chinadaily. com.cn/english/doc/2005-06/08/ content_449612.htm (February 8, 2010).
95–96 "Pelé's Son Says He Is Free of Drugs," notiemail.com, June 5, 2007, http://news.notiemail.com/ noticia.asp?nt=10921620&cty=200 (February 8, 2010).
96 *Pelé: The Autobiography*, 276.
96 Ibid., 276.
97 Ibid., 304.
97 Nick Reeves, "Rio 2016 Ambassador Pele Eyes 'fourth World Cup,'" *The Vancouver Sun*, Septtember 30, 2009, http://www. vancouversun.com/sports/2010w intergames/2016+ambassador+P ele+eyes+fourth+World/2052094/ story.html (February 12, 2010).
97 *Pelé: The Autobiography*, 305.

BIBLIOGRAPHY

Harris, Harry. *Pelé: His Life and Times*. New York: Welcome
    Rain, 2001.

Haskins, James S. *Pelé: A Biography*. New York: Doubleday,
    1976.

Pelé with Orland Duarte and Alex Bellos. *Pelé: The
    Autobiography*. London: Simon & Schuster, 2006.

Pelé with Robert Fish. *My Life and the Beautiful Game*. New
    York: Doubleday, 1977.

WEBSITES

FIFA.com

http://www.fifa.com

FIFA.com is an excellent source for soccer information and statistics from around the world.

ESPN Soccernet

http://soccernet.espn.go.com

ESPN's soccer site provides soccer news, scores, and statistics as well as feature articles and video.

goal.com

http://www.goal.com/en-us/

Another excellent resource for international soccer news, scores, and stats.

mlsnet.com

http://www.mlsnet.com

The official site of Major League Soccer, America's professional soccer league.

INDEX